'At many junctures of the challenging process of parenting I've often exclaimed: "Why can't kids come into this world with a 'how to operate' manual!" Parenting is a non-stop rollercoaster, which is not on auto pilot and with every new twist and turn, challenge and accomplishment, comes the realization that even though you think you're in control, you're not! Parenting is team work and the team will listen and understand only if they speak the same language as you. *Who Do You Think You're Kidding?* helps you to understand your role, responsibility, and duty as a parent and most importantly, to connect with the most important people in your life—your children!'
—**Pooja Bedi**

'Lina Ashar uses her years of experience as an educationist to share key insights that can help parents nurture their child's creativity and achieve their full potential. Written in a lucid conversational style, *Who Do You Think You're Kidding?* speaks directly to every parent who wants to prepare their child for adult "life's success".'
—**Satyajit Bhatkal (Producer/Director of *Satyamev Jayate*)**

'*Who Do You Think You're Kidding?* without a doubt will be a valuable tool in any parents' kit bag. Lina, with her vast experience over several years in dealing with kids and their parents as an educationist, is in a prime position to be writing a book on this subject. As a father, my daughter is my life. Reading Lina's book will only enhance my knowledge of understanding my role and responsibility as a father even better.'
—**Ravi Shastri**

'I wish I was back to kindergarten so I could learn from such a loving and caring head of the organization such as Lina.'
—**Jackie Shroff**

'She [Lina] has been a pioneer in understanding that education should be tantamount to play and recreation. I have found her highly cognizant, especially as a teacher and I'm delighted to find her releasing this much needed book on parenting. If all of us would just understand that the mind, the brain and the subconscious must work in accordance for a peak-performance, life will become beautiful!'

—Raageshwari

'It is not rocket science that the formative years of a child are also the most important—not only in what kind of adult the child will grow up to be, but also how this will shape the future of the world and the human race. Educationists, therefore, have a task that is as onerous as it is exciting. Lina Ashar takes on this challenge with aplomb in *Who Do You Think You're Kidding?*, using her expertise to map out a path that will not only alleviate the anxiety of parents, but also inspire them into becoming wonderful teachers themselves.'

—Ayaz Memon

Who do you think you're Kidding?

Parenting in the new age of digital revolution and globalization

Who do you think you're Kidding?

Parenting in the new age of digital
revolution and globalization

LINA ASHAR

RANDOM HOUSE INDIA

Published by Random House India in 2012

1

Copyright © Lina Ashar 2012

Random House Publishers India Private Limited
Windsor IT Park, 7th Floor, Tower-B
A-1, Sector-125, Noida-201301, UP

Random House Group Limited
20 Vauxhall Bridge Road
London SW1V 2SA, UK

978 81 8400 197 6

Typeset in Adobe Garamond by Jojy Philip

Printed and bound in India by Replika Press Private Limited

To my son Drish
who was born an old soul
and awakened me spiritually

Contents

Foreword

As a musician I operate in an environment that is ever-changing, due to its inherent creative nature. No two days are the same, no interaction repetitive. What is incredible is that as a parent it is no different.

All joys aside, it's a very challenging job. My daughter, Bipasha, though genetically my replica, is cut from a very different cloth. It's probably because of the fact that my childhood cannot be compared to hers in terms of exposure. So, she's smarter, wiser, more aware than I ever was. Which is great, wonderful in fact. But also scary.

How do you filter the exposure our children receive? Do you ration it out? Or do you let your child be? Questions that my wife and I struggle to answer on a daily basis. Fortunately for us, her upbringing is not just in our amateurish hands, she has an institution like Billabong guiding her, moulding her. Quite like a surrogate parent.

I believe that *Who Do You Think You're Kidding*, with its expert advice on parenting, is a timely guide for parents to develop their children into leaders of tomorrow.

Shekhar Ravjiani
Music Director

Introduction

LOL. ROLF. TTYL. TC.

Anyone who is up-to-date will know that the above are no longer just acronyms. It's today's language. Love it, hate it, there's no escaping it. In our dizzying lives, we use it to save time and energy. This evolved language is the first indicator that we live in a different age. The world resembles nothing of what we knew of it when we were growing up. The formidable black dial phones, Doordarshan on TV, endless play time, and families of six or even eight are dinosaurs of the past.

Change has never been as accelerated as it is now. What is a new technology today is redundant in a few months. If we think today's world is cutting edge and 'fast', we better think twice because the social and economic world of tomorrow is going to be nothing like we've ever imagined. Can you conjure up the world that is waiting for our children?

I'm sure not.

We as parents cannot exist in our ivory towers. We need to keep up. So in this era of abundant technology and globalization the question arises—what becomes of our children? How do you parent the child in this era of constant flux?

I deal with hundreds of children and their parents, each as different as the next. Yet over the years I have noticed one common thread that ties them all together—their questions. The questions are numerous and varied and they dodge me everywhere, not only as a parent of a now 21-year-old, but also in the role I play in educating hundreds of children who attend my schools.

'How do I handle this situation?', 'How do I prepare my child to be ready for the future if I don't know what the future will look like?'

Then there are other questions. Ones that are new and loaded with today's context.

'How do I know how much Facebook time to allow to my child?' or 'How many hours of Angry Birds is okay?' or 'Is it okay to let my daughter stay out with her friends on a school night out?' or 'How safe is it to upload photographs on the net?' or 'Should I give my 7-year-old a mobile phone?'

Parenting has a whole new meaning to it. Today, the challenge of bringing up a child has increased tenfold. It's not just about your child getting the best grades in school or turning out 'okay', it's about raising a global citizen who is intelligent and aware of his situation and that of others.

I strongly believe that every child is born with an independent blueprint and you will notice it if you pay attention. As a middle child, I have two brothers, the older one a highly intelligent and diligent person and the younger one a brat who grew up paying very little attention to school, books, or our parents. I was between the two in age and in my behaviour. I did what I needed to do to get through school reasonably well but without the diligence and application that my older brother demonstrated. My mom noticed that I spent most of my time with kids younger than myself. She was worried that I was 'mentally retarded' (that's what they called it in those days, when political correctness was not so important.) But soon she realized that I played with younger kids because I loved teaching them. I used to read out entire storybooks to them even before I was formally instructed in reading. She figured out that I was 'reading' the story from memory because when she would ask me to read from somewhere in between, I was unable to. I would have to turn back to the first page.

As I grew up, teaching became my passion and I soon graduated to be a teacher in Australia. My entire focus was on how to capture the imagination of children who would not usually be interested in 'high end' content. When I explored literature for my students, it was with the understanding that very few children, enjoy the web of words. For most other children, especially boys (because of the different make-up of the brain), literature has very little functional meaning in their daily lives. I started using Cyndi Lauper's 'Time after Time' or Simon and Garfunkal's 'Sound of Silence' as poetry instead of Keats or Yeats and noticed that it all started 'happening for them'. It was that understanding that led to my vision of Billabong High and a 'commitment to colourful learning'.

What I found was that when students found a link between learning and real life, it seemed to increase student motivation and, therefore, helped in the development of skills or strategies that make a student more competent. In this environment, I found that students were able to take ownership of their own learning. Fortunately, many of the strategies that 'empower' and 'engage' students also lead to increased motivation. As students become engaged in learning, they begin to discover the relationship between effort and success, between success and motivation, and start to develop a higher sense of self.

Failure is not motivating. Success is motivating and allows children to develop their confidence and competence. So, as much as possible, we must take advantage of the child's talents and interests in order to motivate them. Children will continue to achieve their goals if they see the relationship between the learning process and its outcome. After initially tasting success with poetry in song, they will be more likely to succeed with Keats or Yeats.

At the age of 23, I met an Australian boy and was infatuated with him. My parents were aghast. They strongly believed that every good Gujarati girl should marry a good Gujarati boy. So they manipulated me into coming to India, convincing me that if our love was true we would be together nevertheless. Their devious ploy worked out—my trip to India changed my life.

I joined a prestigious school in Juhu and became a teacher to a class of 55 students. The system was totally based on rote. My Australian teacher friends were perplexed when they found out the grade levels I was teaching. Didn't Indian schools know that teacher training for pre-school children, primary school children, and high school children was completely different? Not really, I told them because the way we were supposed to teach primary school students was similar to how a teacher would approach older students.

No one seemed to comprehend that children cannot think abstractly till about 9 years of age.

The system did not allow kids to learn concepts because the focus was on memory.

I intuitively knew that memorizing any information that the brain cannot connect to in a meaningful way was not only difficult, but also highly stressful. Today, we know that memorizing is the lowest level thinking skill. Bloom's Taxonomy of Learning today validates the perceptions I had about memory and its associated stress levels. The fact is that the more disengaged (figure 1) the brain feels from what is being memorized, the higher the stress, and the lower the contribution to the development of the brain. The other fact is that when the brain is forced to commit things to memory in this manner, it goes into short-term storage to be deleted once the brain sees no further use for it, usually post a test or exam.

Figure 1: Bloom's Taxonomy of Learning

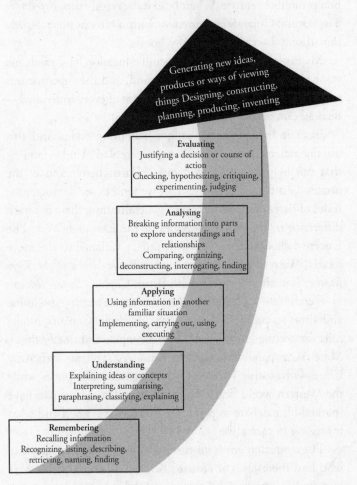

Generating new ideas, products or ways of viewing things Designing, constructing, planning, producing, inventing

Evaluating
Justifying a decision or course of action
Checking, hypothesizing, critiquing, experimenting, judging

Analysing
Breaking information into parts to explore understandings and relationships
Comparing, organizing, deconstructing, interrogating, finding

Applying
Using information in another familiar situation
Implementing, carrying out, using, executing

Understanding
Explaining ideas or concepts
Interpreting, summarising, paraphrasing, classifying, explaining

Remembering
Recalling information
Recognizing, listing, describing, retrieving, naming, finding

I knew I had to do something about it. This time, I did what my parents wanted me to do. I married a nice Gujarati boy and convinced my dad to loan me money to start my first pre-school. My father, a typical Gujarati businessman, made me draw up a business plan to prove to him that this was going to be a profitable venture. When I did it, he readily supported me. The natural Gujarati entrepreneur within me was born. Slowly but steadily I set up a chain of schools.

My experiences with children and education have made me want to share how the brain, the mind, and the subconscious work together to create the life outcomes of every individual—be it an outcome of success or mediocrity.

Each individual has a unique parenting style. And this usually reflects the way they were parented. Understanding that can help us understand our children better and in the process be a better parent. Usually we tend to see demographic styles of parenting. At the cost of generalization, there is a stark difference in the parenting styles of the East and West. The Eastern helicopter parent stands out in variance to the more relaxed Western parent. Amy Chua's *Battle Hymn of the Tiger Mother* is in sharp contrast with Bryan Caplan's *Selfish Reasons to Have More Kids*. While Amy advocates strict discipline and little scope for a democratic approach, Caplan's model calls for getting kids to learn *from* examples and not *by* them. Most Asian parents may find themselves agreeing with Amy Chua—advocating hard work and rigorous discipline, while the Western world finds its voice in Caplan. These two have sparked off a debate in parenting as to what is good and what is missing in each style.

The confusion arises for parents in the Indian metros today who find themselves at crossroads. The influence of the West in daily life is high and I've observed that parents seem unsure as to what to teach their children. Style statements seem to be originating from young and hip channels like Channel V or MTV. Breakfast today consists of cornflakes or oats. Traditional food items like poha or parathas are making less of an appearance on our kids' plates. Mumbai is confusing, as a city, to many parents. Traditional values are offset by modern points of view in the same city. The suburb of Bandra is very Westernized while the suburb of Vile Parle is still strongly rooted in tradition. Bandra is the hub of shopping, especially for Western apparel, while Vile Parle is a paradise for traditional Indian clothes. The trendiest bars and pubs, fine dining restaurants, and street food, it's all available in Bandra, offering not just cosmopolitan cuisine, but a cosmopolitan experience too. Then there are Indian parents raising their children in the West. These parents seem to be caught in a time warp and want to raise their kids exactly like they themselves were raised in India, and impose severe restrictions on them. All my Australian friends went to and hosted sleepovers, but I was never allowed to stay out overnight. My father was livid the day he found out that I had worn a bikini. The internal and external conflict of how to parent is interesting and intriguing—internally as a constant psychological debate and externally between individuals who are so often the parents themselves, each believing that their style of parenting is superior.

Parenting a global citizen requires a global approach. The future is as unknown to a parent as it is to a child. Experiences of our parents and grandparents may not suffice as they were parenting for stability and conformity. What worked for your parents may not work for you! We are parenting for non-conformity. Today, parenting needs to be customized and personalized. Thus, there is no sure shot formula. It is a combination of family background, financial strength, social orientation, but, most importantly, the beliefs of the parents. So while you may let your kids choose their books, games, food, and clothes, you may find the need to regulate social manners and safety concerns. Teaching kids to have appropriate social behaviour has always been the prerogative of a parent. Parenting is a matter of walking the tight rope—being both taut and subtle.

Just as any major economic or social change has an implication on every aspect of life, globalization and the digital revolution have not only changed the way we work and play but also the way we educate and parent our kids. This generation of children need to be geared to do more right-brained tasks that involve creativity, problem solving strategies, communication, and emotional engagement. This, in turn, demands a major shift in the way the Indian education system works and what parents deem important for the child to learn. If our schools continue to focus on mathematical, analytical, and mechanical abilities that are rapidly being replaced by Google, machines, and technology and as parents we continue to value and perpetuate that focus, we Indians may end up as the back office of the Western world. I meet scores of Indian students who are brilliant academically and yet will struggle to make it big once they're out of school. A CBSE topper who scored 100 percent in Class 12 in an English exam stated in an e-mail to *Outlook*: 'It all depends on how one pen down the ideas… The flow in the language helped me fetched marks'. (sic)

The criterion for success has changed. We have moved from a Knowledge Age to the Creative Age. Simply 'knowing things' does not serve any purpose. We have Google for that now. Getting 100 percent in a written paper is of no use if the child is unable to apply knowledge in daily life. Schools and parents have to work together to ensure that the child turns into a learner for life.

Gene N. Landrum in his book *Entrepreneurial Genius: The Power of Passion,* quotes Andrew Hacker, Professor of Political Science at Queens College: 'On the whole, most individuals (with high IQ levels) will peak during their academic years or perhaps during an initial job they receive on the strength of test results. However, after that they will soon be surpassed by individuals who possess more applied forms of intelligence that are not revealed by the test.' He also discusses American psychologist Paul Torrance who says that above 115 or 120, IQ scores have little or no bearing on creativity. Creative genius may be found anywhere along the scale except possibly at the bottom. In a University of California study, Frank Barron researched the influence of variables such as innovative success. He asserts: '…for certain intrinsically creative activities, a specific minimum IQ is necessary to engage in the activity, but beyond that minimum, which is surprisingly low, creativity has little correlation with scores on an IQ test.'

Our focus should be to prepare our children and youth for adult life success. Success tomorrow will depend on how our children ultimately make use of the knowledge and information that they receive today. How we educate our children may prove to be more important than what we are educating them. We need to teach them to tap their innate greatness. We need to hone the right-brained creative skills in our kids. We may soon become a country of BPOs if the focus of education continues to remain on high grades with no thinking involved. The NCERT recently deleted cartoons from its textbooks saying that they are politically insensitive. Every state wants certain opinions and points of view to be fed in its schools. Such politicization of education will ensure we create a nation of non-thinkers.

Only a change in parenting style can make our children global citizens. If we want Indian children to be global citizens, we have to ensure that our kids have a world view of India and how the world looks at us. The child needs to develop an attitude that will rise above regional and religious identities. The child needs to be a global citizen first, a Maharashtrian and a Hindu later. For this, the parent has to keep the doors and windows of his mind and home open to cultural influences of all kinds. He needs to avoid discriminatory remarks against any community or religion. The experience of a world society at home will remain in the subconscious of a child while dealing with people or instances at a global level.

Why this book?

Sachin Tendulkar's son and daughter attended Kangaroo Kids. I was chatting with him one day and asked him what he attributed his batting skills to. He said his grandfather's trick of tying a ball to the door frame and hitting at it allowed him to see what a ball was going to do the moment it leaves the bowler's hand. The hours of practice of visually 'tracking' the ball in his childhood allowed him to 'read' the ball earlier than other batsmen do. Speed reading has the same premise. We begin by giving children beads to move from one end (the left) to another (the right); in the process they are tracking with their eyes, the first step to reading. The faster you track, the faster you read words.

I began workshops and orientations at my schools so that parents would begin to understand the brain research we do to keep our classroom methodology of learning, but I always wished I could share it with parents whose children don't attend my schools.

I decided to write this book a couple of years ago. My usually emotionally connected and considerate son went 'haywire' as most teenagers do. Sleeping long hours in a room which was a complete pig sty, procrastinating with school work and smoking! I was able to cope with this stage because I understood what was actually happening scientifically to his brain. My parents complained, Drish's father complained, his cousins complained. I was calm through it all thanks to my understanding of neuroscience. I knew the prefrontal cortex in his brain was going through a major re-haul! (The prefrontal specializes in attention, judgement, planning, impulse control, follow through, and empathy. While this realignment takes place in the teenage years there is lower activity in the prefrontal cortex leading to short attention span, impulsive behaviour, a lack of clear goals, and procrastination.) I knew Drish would be okay and I assured everyone around me that Drish as we knew him would reappear once his brain was ready. I grew up anti-smoking, I got my chain-smoking Dad to quit and yet what did I do when my brain was in chaos? You guessed it. I experimented with smoking! I know many parents would feel a lot calmer and more in control if they were armed with the knowledge of teenage brain chaos. They will be better equipped to deal with their teenage children once they know that the phase is temporary and 'this too shall pass'. So while writing this book, I have tried to link brain science to ages and stages of behaviour as far as possible.

This book comes as a result of my studies and research in breain science and, how positive thinking and awareness of the subconscious of our children can have a far reaching impact on their upbringing and their life. I have tried to collate research in the field of evolutionary biology, neuro-cognitive science, child development, and my own experiences to create a book for positive parenting. The focus of the parent and the educator today should be to give every child an education that values aspiration over ambition, individual creative thought over rote memory, spirituality over religion, wisdom over knowledge, and the awareness that we now need to embrace a united world over a divided one.

Over the years, a number of studies have been conducted that have examined the relationship between young people's achievement and their levels of development of confidence, persistence, organization, interpersonal skills, and emotional resilience. In addition, areas of positive mind habits that include traits such as self-acceptance, internal locus of control for learning, optimism, non approval-seeking, goal setting, time management, reflective problem solving, etc., are also shown to have a positive impact on achievement. It is possible for teachers and parents to support, encourage, and develop a child's social–emotional–motivational competence and I will explore these with you.

This book is my attempt to help you make the training at home and at school come full circle. Let us create 'a whole new mind', which will bring out the human element in our children, so that we can watch them grow up to be kind and thoughtful individuals. We now need parenting and a teaching that will stimulate the hearts of our children as much as their brains, their spirits as much as their minds. This will be of great value when our children begin to question their legacy—the social footprint they will leave on the world. My sincere belief is that we can ignite human greatness in every child by observing and then nurturing his individual talent. We can provide each child with the tools and resources needed for life literacy.

The 21st Century Child

Children now love luxury; they have bad manners, contempt for authority; they show disrespect for their elders, and they love chatter in place of exercise. Children are now tyrants, not the servants of their households. They no longer rise when elders enter the room. They contradict their parents, chatter before company, gobble up dainties at the table, cross their legs, and tyrannize over their teachers.

Socrates

The times they are a-changin'

It was on a flight back from Australia that I met Pratham.

He was sitting next to me. A little boy engrossed in an article on cars in the in-flight magazine. As he turned each page, he rattled out information aloud about the type of car, cost, type of tyre, engine capacity, and, of course, mileage. He was a walking talking Google in action!

I share great chemistry with children. Just as every man's head will turn if Angelina Jolie were to walk into a room, children turn their heads towards me when I walk into a room! It's just a natural affinity. So it was only inevitable that I'd soon start talking to Pratham.

'Hi, what's your name?

'I'm Pratham.'

'How old are you?'

'Seven.'

'You do love cars, don't you? What else do you like?'

'Well, I love to watch cartoons on TV. Then I play football or cricket on my PlayStation and sometimes iPod touch games. I also play the games loaded in my mom's cell and my dad's BlackBerry.'

Here he paused, and I waited for him to continue.

'But what I love the most is listening to mom's stories.'

'And what kind of stories do you like listening to?'

'You see I am very brave and so I ask only for ghost stories. Di [his older sister] loves fairy tales and all that stuff. But mom can't tell us stories every night. She is so tired that some days she doesn't even have dinner. She just goes to bed once we have finished our homework.'

Our conversation rolled on. I listened with wonderment to his articulate observations and couldn't help but think how well children today gather their thoughts and express their likes and dislikes and even justify their choices with so much confidence. We, perhaps, could reason like him too when we were 7 years old, but we could never make our choices and decisions so independently and then speak about them so confidently... that too to a stranger! Besides, where did we have the voice to claim stakes of our choice? We were told to study this, wear that, say hello, or stay in our rooms. The voice and the choice of our elders were always imposed on us on all matters, arresting the development of our reasoning powers.

My dad grew up in a small town called Tanga in Tanzania, Africa, and he parented me the best way he could. But his parenting values belonged to the Stone Age (only a slight exaggeration). His parenting would have been fine if I was going to settle down in Tanga. Unknown to him, the world that I was going to face had changed and would change even more by the time I grew up. It was my Australian school and university social experiences that gave me the skills I would need as an adult. I remember crying when I discovered that 16-year-olds in Australia smoke. You can imagine what I felt when I found out they were having sex! When I was 16, I visited Bombay for my holidays and that was when I realized that India had completely changed, only that my father was unaware of it. I had to break it to him that not all Indian girls were virgins when they got married. *I* had to burst his bubble!

Today, kids as young as 5 are on Facebook (even though the legal age is 13) and are generally web savvy. Watch a 7-year-old with an iPad and you will feel digitally inadequate.

I did not even know what my phone was capable of until my 7-year-old niece showed me all the cool games that were loaded in my rather antique Nokia set. I gave in to the FB fad and sent my 21-year-old son Drish a request, which he grudgingly accepted (he attributes it to a momentary lapse of reason). I just need to visit his FB page to know that his social world is completely digitally driven. I know who his friends are, where he is partying, what his choice of music and films are. It's all there.

Technology, however, has created a huge generation gap between us and our children—one that is even wider than the gap between us and our parents. To add to that, there is also the pace and extent of change. Once upon a time we wrote and mailed letters. There was time lag between sending and receiving. There was an extended time period, which allowed us to read, absorb, respond. Today the result is instantaneous. Not only are things changing intensely but changing at an accelerated pace. In 1983, we had access to 'mobile' phones. What a change that brought to our lives and work styles. The pace of change has been quick. It's a double whammy. As much as we'd like to avoid it, we have to admit that we *are* living in a different world today. So how do we parent our children in this different world, especially when our views and perceptions are so different from those of our children?

How are children different today?

Let us first see why the perception gap exists in the first place. An example is the simple point of conflict between many parents and children—music. What is music to them can be noise to us. This has a lot to do with the fact that as we age we lose the ability to hear certain tones and pitches. Didn't we enjoy disco and rock when we were kids? And didn't our parents wonder why we were so fascinated by the noise our music made? The sounds have gotten louder and more irritating only because we have grown older.

But besides that, there are three major factors that make the world that our children live in today, different from the one we knew.

The boundless web

The 21st century child is wired to technology and has access to information like never before. While we had only Doordarshan and its limited telecast timings, kids today are exposed to a multitude of television channels and huge doses of information and entertainment. The Internet has brought the world to their doorsteps.

Auro in the film *Paa* says, 'Google se bachke kahaan jaoge?' And right he is. The Internet is almost the only source of information for most children now. Today's children don't need to remember as much as we did. With smartphones and Google, they have access to information 24×7, unlike us who had to commit things to memory. Being connected to information all the time has changed their balance and approach to learning. They need information according to *their* needs.

The range of choice is not only limited to television viewing and Internet usage, but also extends to the larger volumes of brands and consumer products that are available in the market. The loyalty and attention span of the new generation has decreased. What was flavour of the month for us was flavour of the month for years. What is flavour of the month for our children is lucky if it survives a month. Our kids are bombarded with choices and brands. In an extract published by the

American Paediatric Association[1], young people view more than 40,000 ads every year on television alone and are increasingly being exposed to advertising on the Internet, in magazines, and schools. Not only does this exposure contribute significantly to childhood and adolescent obesity, poor nutrition, alcohol consumption, and smoking, it also leads to an over abundance of choice.

As an exercise in awareness, we at our schools often ask children to 'count the ads' on a pre-recorded television series. The children generally only count the ads that are played during the breaks till we draw their attention to all the other ads that

	In the old days	Today
Listening to music		
Watching TV		
Chatting on the phone		
Reading the newspaper		
Playing the guitar		

are being fed to them indirectly through product placements and are used by characters in the stories.

Access to knowledge and information is no longer a problem for children. We are living in a globalized, flat world where cheap and high-speed communication is bringing us closer and within direct reach to ideas and information. Technological skills along with communication and teamwork will be the most important 21st-century skill sets that our children need to master in the current work–life scenario. However, children must be made aware that the Internet should be used only to procure information and never relied upon as the ultimate source of authentic information. They need to know that information on Wikipedia is not always correct. Accessibility to information does not always make it accurate.

This free-for-all information however has its flip side. The Internet today not only ladles out academic information but also plays a major role in the social life of a child. The Adnan Patrawala case is one example of how the Internet can be dangerous. Adnan, a 16-year-old boy, befriended people on the Internet and was allegedly kidnapped and killed by them for ransom. The fact that the accused got away reinforces how careful we as parents should be while teaching our children how to use the Internet. As parents we feel that if our child is at home and on the computer, he/she is safe. But this is where we are mistaken. The web offers social networking sites, which allow strangers to peek into our lives. Keep your ears and eyes open to how your kids are using the Internet.

The increase in the use of computers at home is also a major reason for the reduction in the hours spent by children outdoors. If a child spends all his time on the computer, he becomes isolated from reality. This results in a disconnect with the immediate family, friends, and society. The child will then grow in an island of his own.

Modern family

A typical urban child today is surrounded by a laptop, a phone, and an iPod/iPad. His eyes are glued to the screen, his ears plugged in with music, and his mind wired to the game he is playing. Children today have begun to enjoy socializing in solitude. The social construct of their connectivity is changing. They are more connected to their friends through their machines.

From a time when the entire community took responsibility for the upbringing of a child to a society of nuclear families, we have changed and evolved as a society. From a time when children shared a room with their parents, they've moved on to having a room to themselves at a very young age. Earlier, joint families had many senior members in the family. Thus, guidance and consultations were always a shout away. Today, the fragmented family in its nuclear form doesn't provide this advantage.

Families today also no longer fall into traditional patterns of father, mother, and their kids. There are single father families, single mother families, families where one of the parents is no longer alive, or families where parents share sets of kids from their previous marriages. The disintegration of the joint family has shifted one more base for the children of today. From being dependant on a variety of relatives, they now only have whoever is available.

Research has shown how the average time spent between a parent and child has dropped sharply since the Seventies. In the 21st century, parents are beset by work-related stress and time

pressures, and fewer have supportive kin or neighbours to stand by at the drop of a hat (because everybody is racing against time and deadlines). Children are growing up in a somewhat aggressive environment, where the allure of drugs, alcohol, cigarettes, and consumer products is widespread. Besides, many of the vacant lots and other 'free' spaces where earlier generations were able to play without adult supervision are disappearing, particularly in metropolises like Mumbai or Bangalore.

Hence, traditional rules of parenting no longer hold water because the profile of parents in the 21st century has changed. But what remains constant is the fact that a parent at the end of the day is a caregiver and has the enormous responsibility and benison of raising her child and help him/her to develop into a strong individual who can unleash the potential tapped within.

Competition

How many of us have said or heard people say that the world today is 'so competitive'? And, of course, use the same logic to push our children to excel academically.

There's nothing we can do about competition. It is a by-product of globalization. Also, as population figures increase and resources become limited and more scarce, our survival instinct makes sure we work that much harder to make a mark of our own and to get our own space under the sun. And this we automatically transmit to our children because *children are not born competitive*. They learn it. Most children don't compete till they reach the age of 5 or 6. They also learn to work in groups only by the time they are 10 or 11.

Competition is a double-edged sword. It has its upsides and downsides. Some children thrive on competition while some are happy doing things for themselves. However, it's not as bad as it sounds. Being competitive can be a good thing. A healthy competitive spirit can bring out the best in a person. Competition helps kids to be aware to what is happening around them. Competition:

- involves decision making, discipline, self control, and maturity;
- teaches kids to set long term goals and work towards achieving them;
- helps them to develop problems solving skills;
- encourages participation;
- develops competency areas; and
- ensures that a child doesn't become complacent.

'Competition can enhance or reduce motivation, depending on how it is used. It is good for some, but it may result in a

Rewarding Competitive Behaviour

If you have a competitive child, it is essential to reward his/her effort. Here are a few things you can do:

- discuss the importance of doing one's best and setting realistic goals;
- encourage your child to participate in a variety of activities before focusing on only one activity to compete; and
- emphasize on participation instead of winning.

And most importantly, do not relive your childhood through your child. Your child is NOT an extension of you. To quote the psychologist Carl Jung, 'the greatest damage to the child is the unlived life of the parents.'

few winners and many losers. Unmotivated or underachieving students often have difficulty dealing with defeat. Until they are ready to cope with defeat, it is more productive to encourage students to compete against their own performance rather than with someone else's. In recent days, the spate of student suicides, has shown us how dangerous competition, fear of failure, and not having an internal locus of control can be.

Winning or losing for a child is serious business, especially if he is competitive. If competition focuses on the negative aspects such as the pressure of winning, then it does not add value to life and can, in fact, cause physical or emotional injury. If it reduces self worth and diminishes the child's self importance and respect, then it becomes something dangerous and can cause stress and even lead to suicide.'[2]

Along with competition comes stress. Most people suffer from it, and sometimes our kids catch it very early in life. Stress causes a downshift in the brain's ability to perform. As parents, we need to provide our children with the tools for handling competition in such a way that they know how to manage the stress caused by it.

Managing Stress

One of the tricks to manage stress is by teaching children techniques to achieve calmness at times of anxiety. I teach kids how to monitor their breathing. I tell them to keep their palms on their stomach and study how they breathe. They should be able to feel their stomach protrude when they breathe in and contract when they breathe out. By learning this, they will be able to calm their stressful energy. This technique works well for adults too.

Self-esteem

Another important thing to teach children, while they are learning to handle competition, is how to develop their self-esteem. Self-esteem is about how a child feels about himself. If he feels confident and good about himself, he has a healthy self-esteem. But if the child feels that he can never do anything right, he suffers from low self-esteem.

Children do not have a direct measure of themselves. They create a construct of their 'self' from how people react to them. So, their self-esteem depends on how and what you tell your child. When they receive the message that they are good at doing things and are perceived as successful individuals, the subconscious mind registers this and tells them the same. If a child is constantly told that he/she is not good enough, the subconscious mind saves the negativity and the child ends up having a poor opinion about himself/herself. This negative impression will thwart the child's progress as an adult.

Increasing levels of competition, reducing paradigms of space and time, evolving sources of information and entertainment, changing moral, social, and religious values is leaving us with an unknown future. The dilemma that every parent and teacher faces today is—'How do I use the tools I have to prepare children for a future that I don't know anything about? How do I prepare them to resolve issues that have not yet risen? What is parenting in this age of digital revolution and globalization?'

These are the questions I seek to answer in this book.

Subconscious Programming

If you change the way you look at things, the things you look at change.

Dr Wayne W. Dyer

The hidden mind

For some reason I grew up frightened of moths. A moth could be in the other side of the room, 20 feet away, but it would still cause extreme anxiety, palpitations, and intense fear in me. Also, the moths in Australia are much larger than the ones in India. My rational mind grappled with it for a long time. 'Lina, how can you be scared? Moths are harmless. They cannot hurt you at all.' Or 'You are not scared of butterflies so why are you scared of moths?' 'They are just dark butterflies.' I tried everything but I could not shake off the fear each time I saw one.

Two years ago, when I first became interested in subconscious programming, I came across the American psychiatrist Brian Weiss's work and started reading his book *Through Time into Healing*. His research includes reincarnation, past life regression, future life progression, and survival of the human soul after death. As I was reading and experimenting with regressive therapy and talking to my father about all of this, my father suddenly connected the dots and exclaimed, 'Do you remember the time when you were stuck in the bathroom with a bat?' He went on to remind me that when I was 7 years old I got stuck in the bathroom with a bat that had found its way in. My dad found me sitting in one corner, petrified and frozen, with the bat flapping around me. I have no memory of this occurrence as the human brain is wired to suppress painful memories. I realized that I had internalized this fear and that it surfaced every time I saw a moth.

The important point to note is that the subconscious mind is not good at distinguishing between a real physical threat to our physical self and a perceived threat to the image we have of our self. This perceived image is known as the ego in psychological language. This is where the fear of failure can sabotage our chances of success.

To demonstrate how the subconscious mind works, I often tell children this well known story of two salesmen who were sent to Africa to assess the opportunity of setting up a shoe factory. One salesman telegraphed back to say: 'No opportunity. No one wears shoes.' The second salesman telegraphed: 'Great opportunity. No one wears shoes.'

The subconscious mind is the engine that determines our conscious thoughts, the actions we take, and the decisions we make. Both salesmen were looking at exactly the same thing but their perceptions were completely different. This is because, at the subconscious level, one was tuned to complacency and the other to take risks and see opportunities.

Anthony Robbins, who conducts Business Mastery and Life Mastery courses, is a transformational teacher. I attended his 'Date with Destiny' session in Bali in 2011, which turned out to be a complete eye opener. He spoke about the process of reprogramming the subconscious mind and the patterns that form over the years. During the course I realized that as an adult, I always thought that my decisions were made by my logical conscious mind using the power of reasoning, when the reality is that 90 percent of my decisions are programmed by my subconscious.

The way we perceive things depends on what is stored in our subconscious mind. If you have grown up thinking lack, you will hoard. If you grow up with the fear of failure, you will fear taking any action that has a chance of failure. If you have grown up hearing 'money is the root of all evil', then financial abundance will evade you no matter how much your conscious mind believes and wants to be rich.

The subconscious mind is more powerful than the conscious mind. If the desires of the conscious mind are in conflict with those of the subconscious mind, it is the subconscious programming that will win. If as a child you were repeatedly told or received signals that you were worthless, those messages have been programmed in your subconscious mind. These will undermine your best conscious efforts to change your life and succeed in adulthood even if your conscious mind decides it wants to. The subconscious mind will sabotage any efforts of your conscious mind unless the two are in sync, or if you can find a way to reprogramme your subconscious brain. In simple words, if our subconscious brain believes we don't deserve success or love or happiness, we will keep sabotaging our conscious efforts to achieve any of these.

The significance of this information is huge for parents. Given this understanding of the constant download into our subconscious brain, imagine the consequences of hearing a parent say: 'you are a stupid child' or 'you can't do anything right'. *Parents need to know that we programme our children with verbal and non-verbal communication. Our children will acquire their first perception of self, positive or negative, directly from us.*

Positive affirmations

Roan, aged 6, was upset and refused to go to school no matter how hard his mother tried. The culprit was his math test. He got one sum 'wrong'.

Roan's mother was baffled by why her son, who loved school, suddenly did not want to attend anymore. For little Roan, who was used to getting all his sums right every time, to get something wrong was highly detrimental. He subconsciously felt that he had let his mom down. Unknown to his mother, Roan had been programmed for perfection; she wanted perfection in everything she did in her day to day life. Roan's mom carried this trait from her childhood where she had been taught that anything less than perfect was unacceptable.

'Raul! This painting is really shabby. The colours are all over the place. When will you learn to be neat?'

That is Raul, a 4-year-old boy, being criticized for not being perfect in his work. He was not encouraged for the effort that he put in. Later, after constantly being exposed to such feedback, I found out that Raul stopped painting all together and developed the fear of not being able to do a good job.

Mark Twain once remarked: 'Keep away from people who belittle your ambitions. Small people always do that, but the really great make you feel that you, too, can become great.' And I couldn't agree more. Many of us as adults live scared of failure because of the programming we have had when we were children. We are either scared to fail or play it safe by choosing the conventional path to avoid making mistakes. We avoid taking risks. Our subconscious mind programmes our conscious mind to feel it is better not to have tried than to have tried and failed.

Our perceptions can alter reality

What we are told about people, situations, and places often cloud our mind and our approach towards them. An independent research study was conducted with individual teachers being told that a given class (A) and another class (B) were segregated according to the aptitudes of the students. The only difference being that what they were told was reversed, so the students scoring the higher academic scores were labelled 'mediocre' and the 'mediocre' class was labelled 'high achievers'. What actually happened is that the mediocre group of students began scoring higher grades and vice versa. A teacher's perception of a child can also affect his academic outcome.

This is true for both Roan and Raul. As long as their programming by parents and teachers creates fear, it will not serve them in their childhood or, later, adult life. The words reinforced in Roan's mind are 'fear of imperfection'. In Raul's mind he is 'careless' so there are chances that he will grow up to be careless, even if he and his mother wants the opposite to happen.

Raul's mother approached his teacher to discuss her son's progress. The teacher told her how Raul needed to change his perception about himself and his studies, for which, she needed to change her perception of her child first. A few weeks later, I met Raul's mother and she had a different story to tell.

'I began by telling him that painting is what mattered; not painting within the lines. I told him that getting things incorrect was okay and we could always try again till we mastered them. I was careful not to use words like "careless" and "clumsy" while talking to him. The change was gradual but definitely visible. He became a more confident child, unafraid to attempt things.'

This is a very important lesson for parents, teachers, and educators of the 21st century child. *Positive affirmations infuse the child with positivity and enthusiasm to do better*. If we've grown up with negative traits, which we are aware of and constantly try to eliminate them, they only reinforce those characteristics. Instead, we need to focus on how to develop and foster the positives, which will go on to enrich our life.

Most of us carry the burden of our childhood experiences into parenting. Roan's mom grew up in a family that never accepted imperfection. She believed that it was the right way and continued to implement it in her parenting approach.

Self-limiting beliefs caused by assumptions from one's childhood limit us from reaching our full potential; they stop us from being as successful and as happy as we'd like to be. A limiting belief acts like an anchor that weighs us down and does not allow us to move forward. Limiting beliefs are stored in our subconscious mind and are often hidden from our conscious awareness. We usually experience them when we want to step outside our comfort zone to do something new and challenging.

When explaining how this works with my students, I use the concept of the shackled elephant. An elephant calf in the circus generally has one of its hind legs shackled to a chain. In the beginning it tries to break away, but because it is not big or strong enough, it remains in its place. After a while it goes only as far as the chain allows. When it grows up it is easily in the position to break free of the ankle chain, but it never challenges boundaries because it believes that it cannot break free based on the habituation it has learned when it was young. We can learn a lot from it.

Encouraging an authentic sense of self

We need to show our children that the way we grow, change, and develop through life are strongly influenced by the choices we make. Our children need to have a strong sense of 'the kind of me I'd like to be'.

When I was growing up my mantra was 'to be the best teacher', then my mantra transformed into 'wanting to redefine and transform education in India'. I encourage all children to have a personal mantra that is authentic but can evolve when required. This personal mantra acts as a roadmap to where they would want to go. To make it a commitment to themselves, I ask them to write the mantra down. The Beatles, when they were just a garage band had a mantra to be 'Bigger than Elvis'. I often talk to children about not following the herd and succumbing to peer pressure. When one follows the pack, one is rarely true to oneself.

We need to parent our children to recognize and celebrate the unique beauty within themselves and others so that they become RESPONSE-ABLE—able to consciously and mindfully choose behaviours prompted by a deep sense of being connected with all of life rather than those prompted by a sense of self as being separate. We need to encourage our children to see the 'oneness' of the universe and to understand the interdependency of all living things.

Empathy

At the age of 12, I cut myself with a kitchen knife. I naturally went to my older 16-year-old brother with my blood splattered hands. He just shrugged and went about doing whatever he was doing. My younger brother, who was strolling by, rushed to my assistance, got help, and sat by my side, crying at the pain he knew I was feeling. Interestingly, when my older brother was growing up, my mother was more stressed with work and spent less time with him. She also felt more 'emotionally ready' for motherhood while having my younger brother. My older brother grew up largely in the care of a servant, while my younger brother grew up in the care of our mother. I think that has a lot to do with how they turned out.

Dr Lipton, in his book *Biology of Belief,* maintains that genes play a role in who we are but so do our experiences, which encourage some genes to turn on and others to remain dormant. So, two brothers with perhaps a similar genetic code can be as different as chalk and cheese behaviourally.

This made me think.

Can empathy be learnt? Should it be taught in schools and be made just as important a part of the curriculum as math and science?

There is another vital reason we should teach our children to be empathetic. Because of science. Happiness and emotions associated with doing a good deed creates an emotional reaction in our bodies and brain—increasing the production of dopamine. At our schools we link this with our curriculum. For example, in Grade II when children learn about 'senses', they visit a school for the blind. They learn how Braille works and are involved in raising money (through their own labour) and purchasing Braille kits for children. Children get something out of it—something that lasts longer than the great feelings they experience during the act of giving.

Doing 'good' improves a child's self-esteem, and generally makes a child a well-rounded person. But there is also a more tangible, physical benefit to doing good. Doing good can actually improve one's health. Here's how.

It improves your immune system

A Harvard study showed that thinking about generosity, whether your own or someone else's, boosted the antibody levels in the participant's saliva. Researchers made students watch a video of Mother Teresa's work, and they found the antibody levels of the students skyrocket. The increased levels continued for up to an hour after the survey was conducted.

Another study found that **doing something good for someone else releases the same endorphins that are released during exercise**. These endorphins are linked to improved immune and nervous systems.

It can help ease depression

Doing good deeds helps diminish depression. It obviously helps take your mind off your own situation and puts your problems into perspective, however it also helps on a chemical level. Doing good **releases dopamine**—the feel-good chemical that gets released when we do something pleasurable. According to Dr David Hamilton, author of *Why Kindness is Good for You*, dopamine makes us happier so that we will engage in the behaviour that initially released it again.

It increases the length and quality of life

Several studies have found that people who regularly volunteer to help others regularly have **fewer occurrences of heart disease** than people who never volunteer. These people also generally **live longer**.

Moreover, people with chronic pain reported having less pain, improved functionality, and less depression when they reached out to other people suffering with similar pains.

Just the act of smiling releases dopamine in the one who smiles and the one who is the recipient of the smile.

Empathy is inherent to humanity. Newborns cry when they hear other babies cry. In my pre-schools, I have seen so many kids who walk down to the school happily, begin to cry the moment they are left alone with a bunch of crying kids. This is because they empathize.

Each one of us has **mirror neurons**. Mirror neurons are a very recent discovery. According to research, these neurons are fired when we see someone do an action. It makes us feel what the other person is feeling. They simulate emotions for us. Mirror neurons may be the reason why we yawn when we see someone else yawn. When you see a spider crawl up someone's leg, you feel a creepy sensation because your mirror neurons are being fired.

A study in the January 2006 issue of *Media Psychology* found that when children watched violent television programmes, mirror neurons, as well as several brain regions involved in aggression, were activated, increasing the probability of the child behaving violently too. An article 'Cells that Read Minds' published in January 2006 by Sandra Blakeslee in the *New York Times* talks about the research in the field of mirror neurons. In the article, she mentions Dr Christian Keysers, who studies the neural basis of empathy at the University of Groningen in the Netherlands. Keysers says: 'The ability to share the emotions of others appears to be intimately linked to the functioning of mirror neurons.'

According to Dr Keysers, people who rank high on an empathy scale have particularly active mirror neurons systems.

Sandra Blakeslee also mentions Dr Marco Iacoboni, a neuroscientist at the University of California who studies mirror neurons. He found that professional athletes and coaches, who often use mental practice and imagery, have long exploited the brain's mirror properties perhaps without knowing their biological basis.

Observation directly improves muscle performance via mirror neurons. Sportspersons are often encouraged to watch other top players in action. Watching matches live or going through video recordings of other players triggers the mirror neurons to motivate the player to perform like the ones they are watching.

Dr Iacoboni realized that millions of fans who watch their favourite sport on television are hooked by mirror neuron activation. For someone who has never played, say tennis, the mirror neurons involved in running, swaying, and swinging the arms will be activated.

Research suggests that mirror neurons seem to exist so that we can be empathetic. Mirror neurons mean that emotions are contagious. Psychologists dub this as 'emotional contagion', a phenomenon that Harvard scientist Lewandowski describes in three steps:

1. 'Our non-conscious mind mimics facial expressions through our Mirror Neuron System. This system records expressions and body movements of another person's smile or scowl. In response, it signals activity to your facial muscles, causing a mirrored expression on your face.
2. The expression generated by non-conscious mimicry spirals into a corresponding emotion. When you smile, you generate happiness within yourself. When you scowl, you trigger anger.

3. You and the other person will share these experiences until
    you reach a shared emotional state.'[1]

The power to empathize is also important, if not vital, in
leadership as it enables us to put ourselves in someone else's
shoes. Empathy makes the world a better place to live in.
Why do we, then, not tap into something so inherent in
mankind to make the world a better place? It is said that over
a period of time, couples grow to look similar because they are
empathizing with each other and hence copying each other's
facial expressions. 'Over time because of all the empathizing
they are doing, their faces come to look more similar. For
example, if one partner often smiles in a particular way, the
other is likely to copy it—so creating similar patterns of
wrinkles and furrows on the face.'[2]

In our race to create people who fit into the mould, we are
leaving many aspects of human greatness untouched, especially
in our schools. The focus on competition and examination
systems, that pit children against each other, has slowly led us
to create political leaders who are competitive and even ruthless
in their endeavour to reach their goals. If the leaders of the
future need to be empathetic, we need to relook at what we are
teaching our children.

Kids who work in groups are more empathetic and
collaborate and share more easily than others who don't. World
leaders of tomorrow will need to be more demanding in regard
to what they expect from others but also need to be more
empathetic of how they expect their people to work. Only
then will they have the ability to ignite greatness in individuals
within their team and be able to rally their team forward.

The happiness quotient

When I ask parents what they want for their children, I hear many things that range from a 'good' career to abstract notions of success but I rarely ever hear the word 'happiness'. Happiness is important because only when you are truly happy and satisfied yourself can you start focus on other factors outside yourself.

The definition of happiness then may be defined by external or internal factors. If your children observe kindness and feel happiness first hand, they will reach out to help and build a capacity for gratitude for their privileged existence and only then will the empathy begin to develop.

Most of us measure success by the programming we have received as children. Therefore, it is critical that all parents rethink the programming they may pass on to their children. A child is after all a child. And he/she looks up to you for guidance. We, as parents, need to look at what the child has got 'in him' (and use that to develop potential in our children), rather than focus on what has been 'left out'. A child does not have to be born a leader; he can be nurtured into being one. We should not only worry about developing our children into visionaries and activists of the future, but also look to adding to their happiness quotient.

On a flight to Mumbai, I started a conversation with Kumar, a young parent of a 10-year-old daughter, and soon we got talking on the subject of parenting. Kumar works for a multinational educational company. While he was growing up, his parents ensured that he was well informed and honed his skills of logical and critical thinking. They reared a knowledge

The Kindness Hormone

Research has shown that kindness and kind intentions have a positive effect on the immune system leading to an increase in serotonin in the brain. Serotonin is the chemical that gives one a feeling of happiness and well being. It increases our overall happiness quotient, and emotional and physical health. The levels of serotonin increase in the observer of the good deed as well as the doer of the deed.

One way of increasing the serotonin level in your children and building empathy is to do things like celebrating their birthdays in an orphanage—something my mom did for me.

worker. Kumar knows what to do with information once he has it. He is working on integrating the iPad into learning systems in schools. He is, in conventional terms, professionally successful. I wondered if this would be enough for the child of tomorrow who may need to be not just a critical thinker but a creative one too. Tomorrow, a child will not only need to know how to use an iPad, but may be required to use it to create something new. Are we as parents and teachers really doing anything to ensure that?

The future is about life mastery

The answer lies in tapping the innate strength of the individual. Every individual has the potential for greatness. Everyone can achieve greatness and success if they are *ready* to achieve it.

William Shakespeare said: 'Be not afraid of greatness. Some are born great, some achieve greatness, and some have greatness thrust upon 'em.'

Today, there is a huge surge of life mastery classes and books on the subject. From Anthony Robbins to Dr John Demartini, from Deepak Chopra to Shiv Khera, self-development gurus are offering answers to all our problems. Dr John Demartini is one of the world's leading authorities on human behaviour and personal development. He believes that every human being has a set of values. These values arise from a combination of the conscious and subconscious mind. Each person also sets a hierarchy of values for himself. Whatever is your highest value, you will be inspired by. You identify with your highest value. Any time you link what you want to learn with your highest value, you learn it faster.

Our schooling and education has been through a fixed, pre-established system, which does not necessarily link our learning to our areas of high value. Thus, we go through the process of learning without any motivation.

Conditioning

Like many great scientific findings, conditioning was discovered accidentally. 'During the 1890s, Russian physiologist Ivan Pavlov would present a dog with food and ring a bell, causing the dog to salivate. Over time the dog associated the ringing of a bell with food and would salivate on cue. This concept is known as conditioning.'[3]

'Dogs aren't the only ones who react to the world using a series of conditioned responses. You are also conditioned to react emotionally when certain events occur. For example, a boy plays with his mother in the room. A tiny mouse scampers across the floor. The mother screams. The boy is startled and an emotionally conditioned response is set for him whenever he encounters a mouse again, unless it is Mickey Mouse of course!'[4]

'Though mostly by accident and for the most part unconscious, the way we humans react to the world around us is dictated in a large part by a series of conditioned responses we have been learning since early childhood. Conditioned responses are instilled either gently, with repetition over time or as a result of one traumatic experience. And the traumatic experience doesn't necessarily have to be real. Sometimes, a really scary movie can instill a fear of the dark in someone, just as being attacked one time as you walk down a dark street can.'[5]

Most adults will have some habitual pattern of behaviour that keeps them stuck in one area of their life. This set pattern of behaviour usually comes from a childhood experience that has caused some trauma known or unknown to the parents of the child. At the age of 1 when I first tried to walk, it was discovered that I was born with dislocated hips. My parents were forced to leave me in India with my maternal grandmother as I could not

Potential Signs of Feeling Abandoned

- Fantasizing doomsday abandonment scenarios
- Giving the partner too much of everything that he/she wants
- Seeing another person as a threat
- Unreasonable demands on time
- Pulling and pushing the partner away

have received the orthopaedic treatment I required in Tanga. There was born my fear of abandonment that would affect my relationships even in my adult life, causing emotionally dependent patterns and clingy behaviour. Most of our fears and negative patterns come from our childhood experiences. Fear of abandonment is almost always a direct result of feeling or being abandoned at some point in childhood and the resulting trauma of it.

Many therapists work on rewiring such behaviour by accessing the 'inner child' in the adult. The use of this metaphor—inner child—is for the neural networks that store the essence and memory of the child who suffered the emotional trauma; in this case, a fear of abandonment.

The clearing and rewiring process of the subconscious is based on neuroscience. It is more difficult to clear and rewire the brain than it is to programme correctly in the first place. Isn't it simpler then for us to parent and educate our children for life mastery.

Positive Parenting

Parents need to fill a child's bucket of self-esteem so high that the rest of the world can't poke enough holes to drain it dry.

Alvin Price

Patterns and behaviours

There are very few people in the world who did not feel a sense of loss the day Michael Jackson died. Emotions ranged from extreme sadness to anger at a 'life less lived'. I do not wish to focus on the controversy that surrounded his life and his death but instead want to learn from what fractured and tortured his soul, which perhaps led to a life fraught with insecurity and unhappiness in spite of all the acclaim and success.

Michael Jackson seemed to forever want to hold on to a childhood that he perhaps missed out on. He set up the 'Heal the Kids Foundation' with a rabbi from Oxford in 1992. Here is an excerpt from a speech he gave at Oxford University in March 2001 that may throw light on his journey and may encourage adults to view childhood through the eyes of a child. (You should Google his entire speech.)

'Tonight, I come before you less as an icon of pop…and more as an icon of a generation, a generation that no longer knows what it means to be children… All of us are products of our childhood. But I am the product of a lack of childhood… Today, it's a universal calamity, a global catastrophe. Childhood has become the great casualty of modern-day living. Today children are constantly encouraged to grow up faster…The strain and tension that exists in my relationship with my own father is well documented. My father is a tough man and he pushed my brothers and me hard, from the earliest age, to be the best performers we could be. He seemed intent, above all else, on making us a commercial success.'

Michael Jackson had often spoken of his fear of his father, who would watch his sons rehearse dance moves with a belt in his hand. This sort of fear can result in long lasting, self sabotaging and self destructive behaviour. The man who wrote songs hoping to 'Heal the World' could not heal himself. The man who told the world 'You've Got a Friend' died alone. Michael Jackson was never able to heal the fractured inner child within. His time and his actions were controlled by his father. He was not acting out of a sense of self, but simply acting out the designs others had for him, like a puppet.

It is dangerous when children sense that they are being made into an economic unit or that they are growing up dancing to someone else's tune. Such children grow up feeling 'inauthentic' and inauthentic people are not happy people. Unhappy people do unhappy things to others as well as themselves.

There is a reason why I constantly plead with adults involved in the care of children, including teachers and parents, to heed to a 'child's aspiration over their own parental sense of ambition', and why I keep reinforcing that the main purpose of being 4 is to only be 4 and not to get ready for being 25, and why I push for the rights of children to enjoy a stress-free childhood, which includes joyful education.

There are too many children being pushed for perfection all over the world, including India. Children being shunted from tuition after tuition, dance class to tennis lessons, in a never ending quest for perfection.

While deciding what will work with your kid, ask yourself:

1. Am I behaving like this because my father/mother behaved with me in this manner?
2. Am I behaving like this because I believe this programme will work for my child?
3. Did what my father/mother do as parents work for me?
4. Did I appreciate his/her decision then?

5. Was I happy with that?
6. Am I sounding like my father/mother?
7. Am I responding more out of habit?
8. Does the situation warrant the punishment or am I doing it because that's how it's always been done?

In this increasingly competitive world, children seem to be losing the right to joyful childhood, unconditional love, and a life where they are allowed to be aligned to their purpose of being. Our children should find their purpose with our guidance and discussion but without our interference and our ideas being forced on them. Children who are allowed and encouraged to live on their own terms grow into adults who have an enriched life full of joyful expression.

As parents and teachers if we are looking to raise healthier, happier and more successful children, we need to reflect on our messages and actions that will affect our children's emotional, mental, and physical health, for good and bad.

I was recently in Bhopal talking to parents about behaviour modification. A parent in the audience commented, 'I really like your policy of not punishing kids. I practice the same at home. So what I do when my son does something naughty is that I stop talking to him. My dilemma is that I don't know when I should resume conversation with him, depending on the gravity of the act.'

I was aghast. I asked, 'Is your question only a question asking for my advice on the punishment befitting the crime?' She turned silent, as she realized the impact of what she was doing.

The fact is that most parents do what they feel is in their

The Amygdala Hijack

As cavemen, the amygdala protected us as it triggered a 'fight or flight' response and reaction. An amygdala hijack occurs when we respond out of measure with the actual threat (recall my moth story) because it has triggered a much more significant emotional threat. For instance, the amygdala will react similarly to the threat of being eaten by a tiger or the threat of not being able to escape a bat in the bathroom (physical threats) and the threat of an ego attack (emotional threat) such as the fear of withdrawal of love or abandonment by bringing on the flight/fight reaction. 'When one experiences an amygdala hijack, the amygdala overtakes the neocortex [the thinking part of the brain] and there is little or no ability to rely on intelligence and reasoning.'

The immediate result of an amygdala hijack is a decrease in working memory. A great shot of adrenaline is released into the bloodstream, which lasts for about 18 minutes. This surge of adrenaline released into the bloodstream takes 3 to 4 hours to clear.

It occurs in less extreme situations too. If for example your child hides behind a door and yells 'Boo!', the fear surge that occurs is associated with increased activity within the amygdala.

child's best interest. The problem occurs when there is no process of reflection that guides what they feel. Let us take the impact of this mother's 'silent treatment', which is something I am familiar with in my own upbringing. My father, who I share an intense bond with, would stop talking to me every time I did something that he did not like. I perceived this as a withdrawal of love and it caused me a great deal of pain. So I would then keep trying to woo him back.

In a child's mind, withdrawal of interaction or attention is akin to withdrawal of love and affection. My father, like the Bhopal mother, was doing the best he knew with the tools, resources, and knowledge available to him at that time. The point is that all of this fear is already downloaded in my subconscious and it moulded my adult relationships. When I was married I repeated this pattern. Every time my husband and I had a disagreement I would have an amygdala hijack (see box)—a foreboding that love was about to be withdrawn, and I would give into his demands. I couldn't set any boundaries in the relationship. Given my research and knowledge I knew not to repeat the pattern with my son.

Imagine the consequences of the patterns that are set through our childhood. Imagine downloading perceptions we receive intentionally or unintentionally of being unworthy, or stupid, or incapable. The messages that we learnt become absolute truths that will shape us behaviour throughout our lives.

The questions might be uncomfortable but ask yourself:

1. Do I use the same techniques that my parents used with me?
2. Do I belittle my children the way my parents belittled me?
3. Do I make my children feel guilty the way my parents made me feel guilty?

4. Do I withhold love the way my parents withheld love from me?

The aim of these questions is not to condemn what may have happened to you as a child, but instead to relook at your childhood, which will help you to gain a perspective on what your ultimate parenting aims for your child should be.

People who are successful in life seem to have one thing in common. They all seem to be doing something different and special with their neural network to maximize their potential and achieve their goal. Research has shown that every time you think a thought, feel an emotion or execute behaviour, there is always some sort of corresponding change in your brain. In some instances we can detect these changes in the brain's physical landscape. 'For example, London black cab drivers have regions of the hippocampus—an area of the brain involved in memory and spatial navigation—that are considerably larger than that of the average person.'[2] Research by Eleanor Maguire and colleagues at the University College London suggests that these cab drivers started out with fairly ordinary brains. But when motivated to commit routes to memory, they literally built a better brain, neuron by neuron.

This is true for anyone, including you, if you put your mind to it. The news is exciting for parents in terms of parenting strategy. **We should train our children to drive their thoughts and emotions in positive ways.**

We learn the most from the stories we encounter. There is a Native American story I love to tell kids about the power of our thoughts creating patterns and leading to the outcome of our lives. It is the story of an old Cherokee chief teaching his

The Master Thief

I believe this Grimm's fairy tale shows the value of developing positivity.

One day an old man and his wife were sitting in front of a miserable house, taking a break from their work. Suddenly a splendid carriage with four black horses came up to them, and a richly-dressed man descended from it. The peasant stood up, went to the great man, and asked what he wanted, and in what way he could be useful to him. The stranger stretched out his hand to the old man, and said, 'I want nothing but to enjoy a country dish for once.' The peasant smiled and said, 'You are a rich man, but you shall have your wish.' The wife went into the kitchen, and began to wash and rub the potatoes. While she was busy with this work, the peasant said to the stranger, 'Come into my garden with me for a while, I still have something to do there.' He had dug some holes in the garden, and now wanted to plant some trees in them. 'Have you no children,' asked the stranger, 'who could help you with your work?' 'No,' answered the peasant, 'I had a son, it is true, but it is long since he went out into the world. He was a ne'er-do-well; sharp, and knowing, but he would learn nothing and was full of bad tricks, at last he ran away from me, and since then I have heard nothing of him.' The old man took a young tree, put it in a hole, drove in a post beside it, and when he had shovelled in some earth and had trampled it firmly down, he tied the stem of the tree above, below, and in the middle, fast to the post by a rope of straw. 'But tell me,' said the stranger, 'why you don't tie that crooked knotted tree, which is lying in the corner there, bent down almost to the ground, to a post also that it may grow straight, as well as these?' The old man smiled and said, 'Sir, it is easy to see that you are not familiar with gardening. That tree there is old, and misshapen, no one can make it straight now. Trees must be trained while they are young.' 'That is how it was with your son,' said the stranger, 'if you had trained him while he was still young, he would not have run away; now he too must have grown hard and misshapen.' 'Ah, father,' he said 'the young tree was bound to no post and has grown crooked, now it is too old, it will never be straight again. How have I got all the wealth you see? I have become a thief: whatever I desire is mine.'

grandson about life. The chief talks to his grandson about an internal fight that exists inside people—a fight of two wolves. One wolf is evil and is all about anger, envy, sorrow, regret, arrogance, lies, guilt, resentment, and self-doubt. The second wolf is good and represents joy, peace, love, generosity, truth, serenity, compassion, hope, and faith. He says that all people, including his grandson, will experience the internal battle of the two wolves. After pondering for a moment his grandson asks, 'Which wolf will win?' The grandfather says, 'The one you feed.'

Positive parenting stems from having a positive approach. Most people discover the strength of positive thinking and mind training when they are adults. Who says kids can't do the same? If we parent our kids in a way that they are able to train their minds in early childhood, then they will become strong individuals (unlike the young man in the story who became a thief). Positive and negative thoughts are equally powerful. We need to unlearn and relearn new habits of the mind. We need to train our kids to learn the power of the subconscious mind.

Setting goals

'In 1953, researchers surveyed Yale's graduating seniors to determine how many of them had specific written goals for their future. The result: 3 percent. Twenty years later, researchers polled the surviving members of the Class of 1953 and found that the 3 percent with goals had accumulated more personal financial wealth than the other 97 percent of the class combined!'[3]

Simple Tips to Re-train the Mind

- How do you usually put on your trousers? If you use your right leg first, try using the left from today. If you use your left leg first, try using the right from today. Remember, it will take you 21 days to get out of your older habit and into the new one.
- Help kids create mental pictures of themselves having succeeded in what they want to do.
- Teach them to make positive affirmative statements like 'I am happy today. The day will go ahead well. Today I will win the race.'
- Motivate them to send out positive vibrations Focus on what you desire rather than what you don't have. The more you focus on what you don't have, the more you will attract it in your life.
- Teach them to desire something so much that they are self motivated to do what it takes to get it.

Goal setting is not only adult specific. Children too need to set goals to help them move ahead positively. *Goals help children get a sense of direction.*

Nature provides babies with their own goals. The baby has goals to lift its head, turn on its stomach, crawl, walk on fours, etc. There is an age window of development during which a baby naturally develops milestones, such as sitting, crawling, walking. These are what we call milestones of development.

But as humans grow, a sense of direction needs to be set. This is where parents play a vital role. Goals will differ with the age of the child. Your 3-year-old could be motivated to learn how to ride a tricycle, while your 7-year-old could be motivated to learn how to skate or dance. Stick a picture of a skater, or whatever else he is interested in, in your child's room. It will motivate him.

For slightly older kids, ask them to write down their goals. Writing down goals has a tremendous effect on the subconscious. It will serve as a constant reminder of what you want to do.

Creating perspective

Another important aspect of positive parenting is to be able to teach our kids perspective. Perspective leads to empathy and creativity. It's only when we are in someone else's shoes do we think and feel like them.

I recently came across a TED talk by a young man K.K. Raghava, who created an app that changes the story when the tablet is shaken. Stories are narrated from a different perspective with each tap. So the Indian freedom struggle app provides the perspective of India, Pakistan, and the British.

Perspective is essential. One can teach perspective using very simple techniques. Common fairy tales can be rewritten from the perspective of any character. Get your child to recreate the story of Cinderella from the perspective of the prince or the ugly sisters. The recent movie *Snow White and the Huntsman* gives a twist to the tale by narrating it from the hunstman's point of view, as a protector of Snow White. In the same fashion, get your kids to write a story from the perspective of the good guy *and* the bad guy. Other activities you can engage your child in:

- celebrate different festivals. Take them to a temple, a church, and a mosque;
- ask them to list out 10 things they need their mobile phone for. Now tell them to discuss these things with their grandparents. How did that generation handle these situations without a phone? It will put things in perspective for them.

Developing observation skills

A confident child is also one who is observant. Only when a child knows what is going on around him will he be able to see the connections that will guide him to the purpose of his life. Observation if a skill that requires coordination of different parts of the brain. You see, hear, listen, think, concentrate, analyse, dig into your memory, compare and contrast stuff. All this needs different parts of your body and brain to work together.

Discipline

It is important, as far as possible, for children to develop an intrinsic locus of control as far as discipline and motivation are concerned. Self motivated children feel more in control of what happens in their lives. This process, however, begins if the child feels that he/she is in control of their lives, become which leads to them taking responsibility for their actions. Thus, they develop confidence, which leads to them becoming self motivated. Children who do not experience this take no responsibility for any of their actions, their successes or failures. They always feel that they have nothing to do with it.

I often ask parents to allow children to control some of the aspects of their life that are not going to have detrimental long term affects and to sometimes allow them to experiment with choice. When a child sees that he is not allowed a voice, he blames everyone else for what's happening in his life. He believes the world wrongs him and develops into someone who is always at a constant battle with the rest of the world. Children who have been controlled, much too often tend to see themselves as powerless.

I also ask parents to avoid power struggles as far as possible. A child who is engaged in making limited choices from an early age is unlikely to feel powerless. My advice is to let the child make some choices for himself right from toddlerhood. For example, it is okay for the child to be sometimes allowed to have that chocolate before dinner. Children develop confidence and an internal sense of control if power is given to them in gradually increasing doses as they mature and become more responsible.

Why is there so much focus on disciplining the child?

The focus of child rearing usually seems to begin and end with disciplining the child. This is mainly because we are aiming to bring up a child who is motivated to succeed in life for his own sake.

Children need routine and discipline. In striving to be a friend, we must not let go of opportunities to teach kids a sense of routine and discipline. A rule is a rule, if it involves the safety of the child. No amount of pleading should change the decision of the parent. Thus, as a parent, we need to learn to hold out if we feel the need to. I know of a father whose initial reaction to any request from the child is 'NO!'

'May I have a chocolate?'

'No!'

'May I listen to music?'

'No!'

'May I play now?'

'No!'

The child would then begin to cry and plead, and at times even scream. Finally, not knowing how to stop the child, the father would give in. Soon this vicious cycle became a habit. A 'no' followed by a tantrum followed by a 'give in'. While speaking to this father I asked him if he would give in if the child demanded a knife. He said he would never give in and he seemed to realize what he was doing wrong. At this point I asked the father to think about what the child was asking for before rejecting it. Since a child gains a sense of autonomy and a desire for control as he grows up, the parent may want to process and categorize his decisions into three kinds:

- the unimportant decisions that can be child led (like wanting to eat a chocolate);
- the semi important decisions that may require negotiation and compromise (eating the chocolate after dinner); and
- the critical decisions that require parent dictatorship (the child wanting to play with a knife).

Remember, if a child cannot receive and enjoy attention that is positive, the child will resort to gaining attention that is negative rather than have no attention at all. The trick is to acknowledge all positive behaviour and ignore negative behaviour as far as possible.

Discipline must not be confused with punishment. This is a common mistake that most adults make. Aiming to discipline the child, we often resort to punishment. **Punishment only has**

a negative impact on the behaviour of the child. There is a vast difference between discipline and punishment. Punishment does not make a logical connection between the act of indiscipline and the consequence. For instance, detention in schools is punishment unless the child is engaged in disciplinary behaviour that is tied to the misbehaviour. If a child is given detention for drawing graffiti on school tables, the time spent during detention should be spent cleaning the graffiti off the table. If it is for bullying, then the time could be spent researching and presenting the effect bullying has on the victim. 'Logical consequences make an obvious connection between children's behaviour and the resulting disciplinary action. They cause children either to rehearse the desired behaviour or to restore a problem situation to a more desirable state. For instance, if the rule is "walk" and the child runs down the hall, a logical consequence would be to have him retrace his steps and walk. The act of walking actually approximates the rule, allowing the child to enact it physically. This provides him with a meaningful reminder of the rule to draw from in the future.'[4]

Most schools send students home for being late. In essence, I truly believe, especially with teenagers, that it is far more effective to explore the consequences of their choices than to impose a consequence. Children who walk in late at my schools spend the first period in the library where they write a reflective piece on why they were late and the solutions they can think of to ensure that they get to school on time. This is not a punishment and they understand that because they are in the library. I find students moving towards responsible behaviour when they focus on solutions instead of illogical consequences. Our focus has to be on helping our children be accountable for their choices in a nurturing environment. Remember, punishment does not motivate improved behaviour.

I recall writing to Drish's school because I was furious that he had been sent home for coming to school with dirty shoes! This form of punishment harms the cause rather than helps the cause. I would have expected his teacher to ask Drish to clean his shoes in the school and continue with his day. Being asked to clean his shoes would have not only reminded Drish to come to school with clean shoes, but would also have solved the problem of the dirty shoes. *As parents, we need to view mistakes as wonderful opportunities for our children to learn that every behaviour or problem has a logical consequence.*

At my schools, children are a part of planning the rules and consequences, which I call 'Democratic Discipline'. We find that it gives them a sense of 'ownership' of the rules.

Discipline is:	Punishment is:
Giving children positive alternatives and ways to modify, rectify, or substitute misbehaviour with something more appropriate	Telling the child what NOT to do or taking something away from the child which he values
Acknowledging or rewarding efforts and good behaviour	Reacting harshly to misbehaviour
When children follow rules because they are discussed and agreed upon	When children follow rules because they are threatened or bribed into doing them
Giving consistent and firm guidance	Controlling, shaming, ridiculing
Being positive and respectful of the child	Being negative and disrespectful of the child
Being physically and verbally non-violent	Being physically and verbally violent and aggressive

'Children need positive guidance from adults to distinguish acceptable from unacceptable behaviour and to learn how to behave in appropriate ways. Such guidance is best provided in a physical environment that supports children's decision making, independence, and cooperative interactions. Likewise, a positive verbal environment is the most conducive to children's development of a favourable self-image and socially acceptable conduct.'[5]

As a parent, one needs to be very careful of our own behaviour for this could have far reaching implications on the behaviour of the child.

- **Be happy**: The more emotionally fulfilled you are in your personal life, the better you will be at handling your children. Once you are happy, it will be easier for you to have a pattern in your life, which will be imbibed by the child who is watching you.

- **Make promises; never break them**: If you promise your children something, do it. Don't make promises that you cannot fulfil. If you break your promises, your children will not trust you. And a lack of trust will lead them to question your intentions. Thus, you will sow the seeds of conflict.

- **Walk the talk**: Do what you want your child to do. Avoid anything you don't want them to do. If you throw your shoes over the rack, he will follow suit. If you smoke, you can expect him to do the same. I know of a mother who tells her son that lying is bad and then asks the child to tell her mother-in-law who calls that she is not at home! Children learn from what you do.

- **Encouragement**: While training your kids to skate or cycle, don't shout at them for not getting it right the first time around. Encourage them to try harder and gradually master the skill.

- **Use the 'I mean business' tone:** Be warned that if you yell and shout, your children will do the same. A firm 'I mean business' tone will help you make them get their tasks done sooner.

- **Help children to identify their feelings:** When a child pushes someone while playing a game, we often say, 'No! Don't do that'. We never explain to him why he felt like doing what he did. If you say to him 'I know you are angry', he will realize that it was anger that made him behave the way he did. Thus, as they begin to identify their emotions, they will realize how their emotions control their behaviour. This will help them suitably modify themselves.

- **Clarity in rules; follow up with consequences:** Children can identify empty threats easily. Keep your rules simple and clear. If you have declared certain consequences, follow them up with action. If you don't, children will not value your words. They are more perceptive than you believe them to be.

A positive self image

Observe a baby trying to flip over or beginning to walk. He keeps trying till he finally does it. He never fears failure. But as our kids grow, we put the concept of failure into their heads.

- 'Don't run fast. You will fall down!'
- 'Don't jump on the swing. You could hurt yourself.'
- 'No football sessions till you finish your revision.'
- 'Study or you'll fail!'

Don't the above statements sound familiar?

How many of our parents have said the same things to us? And how many tell our children the same?

Such statements only foster failure. WE put the concept of failure into a kid's mind. Such statements condition our kids to believe that they are not capable of doing things well. This reinforces the negative in them and helps to foster a negative self image. Hence the chances of them failing are higher.

Some kids will think that they are whiz kids while others think of themselves as nothing but failures. A lot depends on the self image that kids build for themselves. Self image is responsible for the levels of confidence that kids experience. When they know and believe that they are good at something and are successful at the task, they begin to develop a positive self image.

While taking pre-school admission, Divya, my colleague, once met a girl who said her name was Sara Don't! The girl had always heard the word 'don't' after her name and thought that was her name!

Try telling your child:

- 'Run! Fast! Take care! You won't fall!'
- 'Enjoy the swing! Take care not to hurt yourself!'
- 'Finish your revision. Your friends will be down for football soon. You sure don't want to miss it.'
- 'Study well. You can do the best courses in the world then.'

Such statements foster a strong positive self image. The child will believe that he can do something if he really tries hard. He will work towards the task with the aim to complete it successfully.

The Bhagvad Gita says, 'A man is made by his belief. As he believes, so he is.' It further says, 'A man's own self is his friend. A man's own self is his foe.'

Motivate your kid to be his own friend and not foe. We as teachers and parents have the responsibility of nurturing the natural interests and gifts of a child over enforcing the most financially viable vocations and professions. Parents who bring up their children with unconditional love and acceptance bring up children with high self-esteem and self-confidence. This self-confidence comes from being allowed to live one's authentic purpose—an inner feeling of the certainty of knowing and living who you are and what you have to offer to the world. It is having the knowledge that you are worthwhile and valuable. We should encourage our children to be aspirational, creating a passionate, exciting, and highly engaging life instead of following the current highest paid job that is always subject to change. I truly believe that passion and purpose leads to success and with success follows financial freedom.

Enterprise education

The development of enterprising skills in young people is important preparation for work and life and is valuable in both school and community settings.

'With persistence and determination, the entrepreneur develops strategies to change their vision into reality.'[6] Growing up in a business family I was surrounded by talk about business and I was often pulled in to work part time in my father's business. This perhaps was the platform that allowed me to create an educational enterprise from my passion for teaching and my skills in understanding teaching technologies. There is a story of a famous entrepreneur who wrote about the time he was 10 years old and decided to set up a makeshift stall outside his house to sell lemonade. He waited for his first customer. No one walked by for hours until his father came along, acted the perfect customer, and enjoyed his glass of cool refreshing lemonade. The child tasted success when he made his first sale and an entrepreneur was born. Interestingly, this story is included in many business study discussions and literature as the Lemonade Stand Business Model. Any entrepreneurial venture is a risk, and as with any risk, there needs to be room for change. By providing students the hands-on experience of running a business, they will be able to make decisions, analyse problems, come up with solutions, and also make mistakes.

Our education system is already set up to provide children with the 'hard' skills they need to go through life; these are the technical requirements of the job. However, we also need to provide children with 'soft' skills such as self-esteem, confidence building, integrity, and optimism to complement the hard skills.

These soft skills are increasingly being sought over degrees by employers and educational institutions such as Harvard Business School (HBS). The managing director of admissions at HBS emphasizes that 'empathy, perspective taking, rapport, and cooperation' are among the competencies the school looks for in applicants. They are placing greater importance on the value of emotional intelligence and interpersonal skills, with the reasoning that to be a successful leader you need to have the ability to think beyond the textbook, beyond the classroom, beyond an academic record.

In the year 2000, UNICEF identified certain life skills that children will need to learn to cope with the rapid changes occurring around them in a fiercely competitive world. These skills include: decision making, problem solving, creative thinking, communication, empathy, critical thinking, coping with stress and emotions, interpersonal relationship skills, and self awareness.

'"Enterprise Education" is learning directed towards developing in young people those skills, competencies, understandings, and attributes which equip them to be innovative, and to identify, create, initiate, and successfully manage personal, community, business, and work opportunities, including working for themselves.'[7]

Tomorrow belongs to the entrepreneur

We need to create and implement a new vision in our children for them to be able to shape the future. Through simulation of mini-business environments in schools, students can have the opportunity to experience 'enterprise competencies' such as self motivation, initiative, and risk taking. An example is a recent programme started by our schools called 'Show & Business', which runs as a part of 'Enterprise Education'. It is designed to equip children with entrepreneurial skills by setting up a fully functioning production house. The focus is on helping students 'sell' their enterprise. The end goal of 'Show & Business' is a professional show created entirely by the children themselves. We hope more schools start to develop entrepreneurial skills in their students. Not only is it necessary and beneficial, but also rewarding and fun for the students.

As parents we can also encourage this at home. If your child is interested in jewellery, encourage him to create a small jewellery business. If your child enjoys baking, help him set up a small bakery business. Begin with a simple balance sheet view. How much funding will be required? How will we let people know of the enterprise? One of our schools possibly has the youngest president and CEO of a company in India! A young boy of 10 and his brother, aged 12, recently created mobile phone applications that have had over 10,000 downloads across the world already. We place a high value on teaching entrepreneurship to our students and these two students are already co-founders and President (Shravan)/CEO (Sanjay) of GoDimensions, a mobile applications firm. The duo has already designed four applications for the Apple store that have been downloaded in over 20 countries!

Change cannot be initiated by children in a society where becoming a doctor, an engineer, or a pilot is still the norm. We must encourage our children to excel in what they are interested in and provide them with the necessary skills to empower them to take up a self-determining approach to achieve their goals. By learning to confidently navigate the numerous opportunities in front of him, a child can obtain a greater sense of achievement. I recall my father receiving a stock of handbags from India in a consignment that he did not know what to do with. I set up a stall at a flea market and sold every piece. Imagine what that did to boost my 17-year-old self's confidence.

Each child is already an entrepreneur. As parents we simply have to be their first customers. After all, the second your child has sold one cup of lemonade he/she has created a business.

Abdul Kalam recently came and addressed students at our school in Chennai. When he spoke to our students, he reminded me of Martin Luther King—two leaders with the capacity to transform a generation with their words. Prior to meeting him I Googled him to know more about our former President. I was excited to know that his vision for education is completely aligned with ours. He says: 'When learning is purposeful, creativity blossoms.' And that is the truth behind any success.

Parenting Styles

Having children makes you no more a parent than having a piano makes you a pianist.

Michael Levine

Your role as a parent begins once a child enters your life. Irrespective of whether you are a father or a mother, parents tend to develop their own styles of parenting. Every type of parenting style has its own reasons and consequences. But what I would like to emphasize is that each of these styles also has its subconscious undercurrents. This is what we need to be aware of.

I will leave you to decide what your style of parenting is. You may find that your parenting style is a mix of many. But the question for the bigger picture is—Are you aware how your style is affecting the subconscious bank of your child?

Diana Barmund, a clinical and developmental psychologist, propagated the theory of parenting styles. She began with three types to which researchers added a fourth. They are:

1. Authoritative parenting
2. Authoritarian parenting
3. Permissive parenting
4. Negligent parenting

These four parenting styles can be put into a chart like a SWOT analysis.

The authoritarian parent

Remember Shah Rukh Khan's father in the movie *Devdas*? That is an authoritarian parent. Strong and adamant, not ready to accept anyone else's point of view, and believes that the child should do things because he said so.

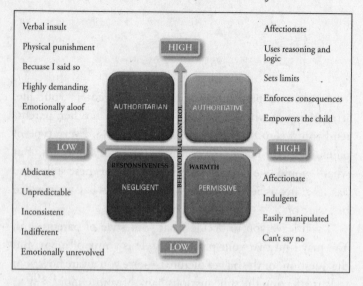

The authoritarian parent likes order, discipline, neatness, routine, and predictability. Children of such parents find it difficult to form meaningful relationships with anyone later on in life. This is because the first relationships in their lives did not culminate in anything meaningful. Such children usually lack self-confidence and stay away from their parents when they become adults.

The authoritarian parent is result oriented and rule based. Parents who follow this parenting style do not hesitate in punishing their child, sometimes even without reason. They believe in punitive measures and not discipline. Such parents do not give importance to the emotions of their children. For the authoritarian parent, the child is only to be seen and not heard. These parents have ideas about how their child should be and the child's early years are spent in trying to live up to the expectations of the parent. The child is rewarded if he lives up to the expectations of the parent. Or else he is punished. Such parents do not discuss things with their children. Captain von Trapp in the movie *Sound of Music* personifies the authoritarian father who raises his children as if they are soldiers in an army.

The paradox of this style of parenting is that children are expected to behave as adults but are not considered such. The child may grow up to be a law abiding citizen, but may not know what to do in life as he has been taught to only obey, never to take decisions for himself. They may lead a very passive life, without ever being proactive.

Bottling up emotions for a very long time can only make children explosive. For as long as they can, children of authoritarian parents may contain themselves. But once they cross their limits of patience, they rebel and may be equally dangerous both to others and themselves. This type of parenting has been linked to adolescent delinquency. Research indicates that children of authoritarian parents have one of the worst outcomes on virtually any measure of social or cognitive competence, academic performance, psychological well being or problem behaviour.[1]

Children of such parents feel unvalued and unheard, and may lack social skills.

The authoritative parent

Remember the parent's role essayed by Anupam Kher in the movie *DDLJ* or the one by Kiran Kher in *Hum Tum*? Both of them are affectionate parents who guide their children through life. They do not lead their lives for them but are their pillars of strength. Such parents are able to bring out the best in their children. Children of such parents are confident, strong, and self assured individuals. They are able to establish meaningful relationships in their lives.

Authoritative parents are democratic and believe that children should have a say in what is happening in their lives. They listen to what their kids have to say. While encouraging independence, they set the limits and consequences for the actions of their children. While stating expectations for the children, these parents ensure that they don't pressurize them to perform. They motivate them so that they perform their best. These parents are warm and nurturing. They allow kids to have and express their opinions and may even allow the children to set their own rules, but will then insist that those rules be followed. They believe in administering fair and firm discipline. The emotional openness that these parents have with their kids makes it easier for the kids to be confident about themselves.

Such parents are able to mix discipline and respect so that children have no ambiguity about how to behave. When there is clarity of action and consequence, it's easier for children to make decisions and think on their feet.

Supportive parenting styles help to foster the development of empathy in the child. Being an authoritative parent is simple. Here are a few things that can help you to be one:

- **Praise positive behaviour:** Parents usually tend to concentrate on how to remove negative behaviour from their children. Instead reinforce positive behaviour with appropriate praise and compliments. Acknowledge small tasks like setting up the dining table, being handy around the house, or fixing up a quick breakfast on a Sunday morning. Hand over a simple 'GOOD JOB!' card or a 'You did FAB!' card and see the difference.

- **Listen before you talk:** Remember all the classes you bunked at college to escape being lectured at? Your child too will run away from you if you fall into the habit of lecturing. Every good conversation starts with listening. Have conversations and not lecture sessions with your child. Understand what their issues are and then give advice or guidance.

- **Show you care:** Kids need to be shown that you care about them. They crave acceptance. Talk to them. Listen to them, cuddle them, hug them, and pamper them, if needed. A little care and affection goes a long way.

- **Help kids to set their own goals:** Keep the goals SMART (Specific, Measurable, Attainable, Relevant, and Time bound). Tell them what you expect. Do not except them to understand because they are of a certain age. 'He is 7. He should know that he has to put his toys away.' How do we expect him to know when we haven't taught him? You should say, 'Raj, I need you to put away your toys away in the next ten minutes.'

- **Stay calm:** A calm parent raises a calm child. If you are nervous and jittery about everything, your child will imbibe the same attitude. Shouting, yelling, and screaming won't help. Such behaviour only undermines the child's self-confidence and teaches him that it is okay to be violent.

- **Choose to discipline with love not punishment:** As a democratic parent, give your child choices and the consequences for any course of action. Let your children learn by trial and error. Demanding a course of action and punishing them for non compliance may hurt them in the long run. They will never develop the confidence to choose between actions and bear the responsibility of its consequences.

- **Let them make their choice:** If your daughter wants to skate without her safety helmet, tell her: 'It's not safe to skate without the helmet. You have a choice: you wear the helmet and have a safe evening or you do not wear it and we go back home to play cards which doesn't need a helmet.' Once you give her the choice and its consequence, your child will also understand the responsibility that comes along with it, and will slowly learn to make the right decisions.

- **Value your child's opinions and preferences:** Sometimes the best ideas come from children but more often than not we are so caught up with our own lives that we don't listen to them. Discuss colours with them when you are getting your house painted. You will have a really bright house if you listen to them. Ask your children to plan out a healthy menu for the week. Children love variety and they will ensure that you have a good menu planned.

- **Remind them that they are loved:** 'I love you'—these three magical words are the cement of any relationship. No child ever tires of hearing that he is loved by his parents. Many Indian parents do not express this emotion. It is almost taken for granted.

- **Modify the way you speak to encourage your child:** Remember that your children will rise or fail to meet your expectations for them. If you express skepticism and doubt, they will return your lack of confidence with mediocrity. But if you believe in them and expect them to do well, they will go the extra mile to do their best.

Child's Age	Say	Instead of
2	'Paint on this paper.'	'Don't paint on the walls!'
4	This is a difficult puzzle but I believe you can crack it if you keep trying.	'You always give up. Can't you finish anything!'
7	'I know you really wanted to win the race and are disappointed you came second, but do you know how many runners came second before they came first. We just have to keep practising.'	'If you had practised more you could have won the race. Haven't I always told you how important it is to practice?'
10	'I know how you must feel at failing the test. Why don't we sit together and look at what we can do to better your next score? Everyone fails a test at some point. What is important is what we do to improve next time.'	'You deserve to fail. You never put the study time in when I told you to.'

Child's Age	Say	Instead of
16	'I know how you feel about cigarettes and smoking being cool and why you experimented. I made the same mistake when I was your age. Then I was lucky that my uncle cared enough to show me how dangerous smoking is. Let us study the consequences of smoking together and also look at how the media brainwashes us into thinking it is 'cool'. I have faith in you to come to the right decision regarding smoking.'	'You will never amount to anything. You always want to find ways to disobey me.'

The permissive parent

'*Kya tum jaante ho main kiska beta hoon?*'(Do you know whose son I am?) How many of us have heard people bring this up in a fight or even in regular conversation? This is a perfect example of a comeback from children of permissive parents.

A permissive parent is usually nurturing and warm but also one who refuses to set limits for the child. They discuss things with their kids, give them choices, and ask for their opinions but they do not set consequences. They encourage free thought without putting much thought into their own actions. They are rather laid back and relaxed when it comes to parenting. They do not demand things from the kids and expect the kids to find a regulation system for themselves. At times it seems like it is the child who is controlling the parents.

Permissive parents are so immersed in fulfilling all the emotional needs of the child that they neglect other aspects of the child's personality. They want them to be a 'child' and hence do not expect them to take up any tasks at home or share any of the house work. Such parents also treat themselves as resources for their children. 'If my son wants a toy, he shall get a toy. He has to be happy.' They are indulgent and do not find anything wrong in whatever their children do.

In an attempt to be democratic and leave children to take their own decisions, such parents do not intervene even when required. Intervention can be to get children to brush their teeth in the morning or a routine for bedtime. They do not

Tips for Permissive Parents

Permissive parents can turn into authoritative parents. They just need to watch their own actions. A little thought into the consequences of their actions will help them.

- Stop and think before you say yes to everything your child asks you.
- Discuss with your child the why, how, when, and where of anything he wants to do.
- Keep track of what your child is doing. If he knows you are not bothered, he will not bother either.
- Decide whether a tantrum needs attention. Think of where over pampering could lead your child.

want to do any of these as they believe that their children will set patterns for themselves and do not need adult help.

The children turn out to be misfits, who are over confident and do not know where the limits of civilized behaviour begin and end. Children of such parents are often bossy and arrogant. They have been used to parents who fulfil every whim and fancy and they carry this attitude through life.

Since they have never been set any limits, they are not sure of how far and how long they can go on. In an attempt to probably discover this, they take their impulsive behaviour to dangerous levels.

The negligent parent

Remember Anand (Anupam Kher) who walked out of his daughter's life in the film *Daddy*. He was a negligent parent. A negligent parent does exactly what the term says: neglect his children. A parent may become negligent due to many personal, emotional, and social reasons. The parent may be an alcoholic or unemployed or just too scared to take responsibility of the child. Children of such parents do not have much respect for their parents. They lack role models and turn out to be disillusioned in life. They are more likely to engage in anti-social activities.

Here are a few scenarios to distinguish how different parenting styles evoke varied responses to the same situations:

Five-year-old Rani pulls Geeta's hair while playing in the garden	
Negligent parent	Doesn't even know Rani is playing in the garden.
Permissive parent	Looks on but does nothing. Believes Rani and Geeta need to sort it out between themselves.

Authoritarian parent	Rani, this is not right. You will not come to the garden from tomorrow.
Authoritative parent	Rani, this is not right. Please apologize to Geeta. Say you are sorry you hurt her.

Sumeet, 13, wants to rent an Adults Only movie and watch it at home	
Negligent parent	Doesn't bother to find out what Sumeet is doing/watching.
Permissive parent	Allows him to rent it when Sumeet begs over and over again.
Authoritarian parent	Sumeet, How dare you even suggest something like this? You will not watch any movies from today.
Authoritative parent	Sumeet, this is not right. We will go to the DVD store and you can rent a DVD that all of us can watch at home. You can watch the movie once you are 18.

Every style of parenting can impact the subconscious of the child. What, how, when, and why you do and say things as a parent makes a lot of difference to what the child downloads and makes a part of his belief system about himself and his capabilities. This download happens with none of the rational adult filters we use. It determines the future course of your child's life. Your style has a lot to do with your own subconscious and how you were reared. So be aware of what you are doing and modify it to suit the needs of this age and your child.

There may be times when each parent has a different style. The father may be permissive and the mother authoritarian. At such times clashes in opinion need to be discussed and dealt with at an adult level, rather than confusing the child with contradictory information. Both sets of parents need to speak the same language. Research shows that children who have at least one authoritative parent are more successful in life than a pair of permissive parents or a pair of authoritarian parents.

You may be a mix of more than one type. Even though there has been considerable research on the styles of parenting and how they impact kids, parenting, at the end of the day, is very personalized and individualistic. You may or may not be a representative of any one style. At times you may be a mix of more than one. So be aware of what you do and how you do things so that you are able to develop a positive subconscious bank for your child.

The omnipresent negligent parent

This is a new category of parent that is developing in the digital age. Today's children are growing up in times when media is all powerful and pervative. Although most of the young parents now grew up in times when television was around, the assault of the medium in daily lives was not so pervasive. Sunday evenings may have been reserved for a movie on TV but otherwise children went out to play. Now, children are growing more and more dependent on screen media for entertainment.

Kids are constantly wired to various machines—on their mobile phones playing games or with the iPad or any other technological media. Believing that this is keeping the child engrossed and busy, a new breed of negligent parents is on the rise. This breed of parents is leaving it to the media to keep their children busy. Parents need to ensure that they utilize screen time to develop creativity in the child.

How is this going to happen?

For starters, parents need to know what their kids are watching. Parents and children should allot time for co-viewing and in this time watch programmes that they can discuss and debate upon later. Plan 'NO TV' days at least once a week and go back to good old activities like a game of Scrabble or chess.

> ### Adman Prahlad Kakkar on Gaming
>
> 'Television is very addictive and is a one-way process. Gaming seems to be the lesser devil of the two. It at least challenges kids to think faster and better than the computer. It is my personal opinion that if games are made less violent, they can motivate children to develop problem solving skills.'

Dinner times need to be totally cell-free times. Challenge the family to a game. Keep all cell phones away and do not pick them up or reply as long as the dinner is going on. The first one to pick up his or her phone clears the table and does the dishes that day. If no one picks up then everyone shares the work.

Schools today are moving towards interactive screen media as a tool of educating kids. The content in schools is highly controlled by curriculum developers and teachers. But that is not the case at home. Unrestricted TV time, no parental control, and lack of censorship on what they are watching can impact the psyche of kids. Unrestricted TV time is a passive activity.

The first thing I ask parents whose kids seem to have an inability to focus is the amount of time they spend watching cartoons. The movements of cartoons are so quick that it hardly gives the brain time to process the information. This can lead to a short attention span. Kids today are growing more violent and also beginning to feel that it's okay to do so. Television programming for children has an increasing dose of violence. Young children do not seem to realise the difference between fact and fiction. Violence on television is depicted in a very life like manner. The fine line between reality and virtual reality can become blurred in the mind of the child. If at any point of time, you are watching a violent show with your child, turn it into a teaching moment. Teaching him what should not happen is a way of converting it. Tell him why one shouldn't be violent. Show him the scenes shown in the programme and explain to him that they are staged and not necessarily true. Explain to him that it's a make believe environment that the television show has created.

Researchers have identified three potential responses to media violence in children.

- **Children succumb to fear**: Children are portrayed as victims. They grow up to fear the world at large. They believe that perpetrators of violence lurk around every corner.

- **Desensitization to real-life violence**: Regular exposure to violence desensitizes children. Cartoons show that violence is fun. This doesn't help children to get a true picture of how dangerous violence could be.

- **Aggressive behaviour**: Children begin to believe that aggressive behaviour is cool. Most of the films portray violent men as heroes who are prone to aggression.

Is parenting an inborn talent ?

My mother believes that the parent of today is just 'overreacting'. 'Why in the world does a mother need a guide to be a parent? A mother learns to care and nurture by herself. It's natural,' she says. She strongly believes that parenting guides give so much information that young parents get confused. Ask any grandma in the family and you will get the best tips from her. When I was a new mum, perhaps my own support systems were laid on similar lines. Then why am I canvassing for the 'How to Parent' industry?

Parenting, according to me, is a work in progress. You acquire this skill gradually in the course of one's day to day involvement with the child by recognizing what works best for the child and for you. That is why this new trend of seeking specialized coaching on parenting strategies and philosophies is the best thing a parent can do. Job commitments nowadays are so high, keeping parents busy that few have time to spend with other families in their neighborhood, engage in long interactions to yield support and advice. Besides, parents themselves may be geographically or even emotionally distant from their own parents and grandparents making asking for advice quite difficult. Paediatricians and other healthcare providers today don't necessarily provide answers to more complex problems that parents might face. At such times, you turn to guide books, magazines, and websites that address the issue from the current standpoint for necessary support.

I believe that you already have the instinct to be responsive, but at certain times even you might need the information and tactics to handle situations. Parenting handbooks and resources can stoke you up to think and come to your own conclusions about what parenting style you are adopting and whether it is proving to be an effective strategy at all. It is indeed a different time that we live in and are faced with different challenges. Accordingly, its strategies have to be different too.

Parental instinct is what makes humans and animals do so much for their children. Some parents find slipping into the role of a parent easy while others may take years to get used to it. For many parents, a new born baby may not elicit deep feelings of love, just curiosity. We are in a country where the mother is compared to a goddess and hence many women find it difficult to accept that they may not feel unconditional love for their child. But it is natural for both the father and the mother to take time to develop a bond with the child.

Bonding can happen over simple activities and starts right from when the baby is born. The more you interact with your baby, the more you bond with him, the more you understand him, and the stronger your instincts are.

Emotional strength is essential in the parent of today to withstand the demands of the child vis a vis societal expectations and their own personal dreams for the child. It is important to take care of oneself to be able to care for another person. Recognize the small and big challenges of your life. Learn to recognize your inner strengths. Tap your potential as a human being to nurture another one of your race. Anticipating and planning for financial security for your family is very essential to live a stress-free life. Be open to help. Strong communication within the family can help you maintain a balanced life.

Hyper parenting

As I see it, our parents wanted to raise children who could fit into their time and society seamlessly. But the parent of today wants to give her child a competitive edge, which may at times border on 'hyper-parenting'. Tuitions begin at a very early age—from pre-schools to IIT, the coaching culture is pretty widespread. Parents are well-meaning but their attempts to provide their children with every possible opportunity by filling up their after school time with music lessons, enrichment activities, and sports crushes the child from within. Children feel suffocated and pressurized due to a lack of time and excessive parental directives. Experts fear that this over-scheduling and over-programming is placing excessive pressure on children and depriving them of the opportunity for free play or just 'hanging out', which is vital for their well being.

Education for most parents today has become a race for marks. Educational institutes and boards regularly reinforce these concepts. There seems to be no other higher purpose of education than studying for exams and clearing papers. Most schools in India still function like a manufacturing unit and build pressure cooker-like stress in our children as they demand hours of extra study sessions to master subjects. It is a sheer waste of childhood, as most of us know that what we rote learnt in school, in isolation to existing knowledge and meaning, went into a short term memory system and got regurgitated for a test and then promptly deleted.

We are not only bringing up stressed out kids, but are also bringing up a nation that will be unprepared for the conceptual age, the age of imagination and creation. It is one of the reasons that my schools place a greater emphasis on higher order thinking skills. It also places an emphasis on fun, which happens the moment you come from a place of high engagement from the child's perspective. Teach any boy math through cricket or soccer and wham!—you have a more patient and willing learner.

The task of parenting, however, is not so simple and things

cannot be labelled as right and wrong. It is to a great extent situational so that either of the styles can yield a desirable outcome or have its pitfalls. Hyper-parenting in moderation can teach a progeny how to acquire self-discipline but if it tips the scale towards extremity, it can stunt their self-esteem and self-confidence too. Sensitive parenting, as long as it is sensibly directed, can bring out of a child an assertive and independent decision taker but if it slips towards over indulgence, it can bring out a brat too. That is why it is preferable to blend both styles for optimum result.

Being an authoritative, yet loving parent alone can produce well-adjusted and happy children. Moderation is the key. A secure attachment to caring parents is the key to laying the foundation of self-discipline and independence, which alone can make children well-rounded personalities. And to that effect, instilling discipline is necessary so that they learn socially acceptable behaviour and etiquette, money management, perils of alcohol consumption or unsafe sex. On the other hand, some amount of indulgence and permissive parenting is equally necessary in matters of socializing with friends, choosing snacks or comfort food, hobbies, following the current trend and culture in dressing or hair cut.

Educational background, financial strength, social class, exposure to other cultures, experience, and aspirations are all factors that shape our parenting styles. And it's simplistic to assume that we can parent our children today the way we were parented yesterday. It is equally simplistic to assume that one style can suit all parent-child groups. What works for one parent and child may not work for another. As they say, different strokes for different folks.

Remember, great parents are made not born.

The Father and Mother Function

The most important thing a father can do for his children is to love their mother. The most important thing a mother can do for her children is to love their father.

Anonymous

One of my favourite authors, Roald Dahl has represented different types of fathers in his novels. In *Fantastic Mr Fox*, he has Fox who is a very caring, nurturing family man who will do anything to feed and care for his family. In *Danny, the Champion of the World*, the father is a single man. In *Charlie and the Chocolate Factory* the father figure is the grandfather. Matilda has a father who cheats people. In *George's Marvellous Medicine* the father is a highly energetic person who works along with his son in trying to create the marvellous medicine. Fathers come in all forms.

Who is a father?

A father traditionally presides over, provides for, and protects a family. In Indian tradition he is called the 'kartha' of the home. Through evolution, mythology, and tradition the father's role has been that of a bread earner. The role of a father today, however, is changing.

Biologically speaking you may be the father of your offspring, but what is it that makes you his dad?

The difference is distinct yet subtle. For a house to become a home, it needs love, affection, and warmth, which can nurture it with devotion and sincerity. Similarly, a father becomes a dad when he has a relationship based on love, affection, and trust with his child. What type of dad you turn out to be depends a lot on what you have been through in your childhood. Practices in-built in your subconscious might make their presence felt. Hence, it's essential to be aware of how and what we do with our children so that their subconscious bank has the best experiences.

Look around you and you will notice that each father–child relationship is different. Sit back and think about your relationship with your father. Was your father friendly? Was he strict? Was he ever ready to help? Or was he always aloof? The relationship with your father can, to a large extent, determine how you as a father shape your relationship with your child.

En route your transition from father to dad, be aware of how your thoughts and actions can mould the character of your child.

The presence of a father is vital in the growing years of a child. Research has proven that a healthy father–daughter relationship is essential for a girl to have healthy sexual relationships in her later years. Sons too are influenced by their fathers. The absence of fathers in the lives of boys often leads them to drugs and violence.

Joseph is a relatively new father. His son is just two weeks old. As much as he is intrigued by the presence of the new person in his life, he is scared about how life will change for him. He feels a sense of responsibility for Joshua, who is tiny and seemingly helpless. Joseph says, 'Joshua needs his mom for everything else, but he finds it easier to sleep next to me than with his mom. I think he feels more relaxed with me.'

This could be true because it's possible Joshua gets more relaxing vibes from Joseph than from his already tired mother. Joseph traditionally might not play a major role in his son's initial phases of life. But, with changing equations Joseph's role too has changed. Dads today not just help clean the baby, but also handle the baby's playtime and help work out his/

her sleeping patterns. Moms work too, sometimes longer hours than the dads. Families are more nuclear in nature. Support systems are not as strong as they used to be earlier. In this scenario, the role of the father has increased manifold.

I am a father. But what will make me a dad?

1. **Touch**: The sense of touch is very strong. Babies realize when they are being held by the mother and when by the father. Young fathers often feel that the baby is too fragile and delicate to be handled and stay away from the baby. This reduces the amount of valuable input you can give your baby about you. When you wrap the baby in your protective hands, he feels secure and peaceful. Lift your baby, carry him, and play with him.

2. **Time**: Rajesh, 44, a businessman, shares a very strong rapport with his teenage daughter. He says, 'In the initial stages, she would be fast asleep when I would get back from work. I would just lie down next to her, hold her hand, rub her little feet and at times even wake her up! We would then play till the wee hours of the morning, when she would go back to sleep, tired but happy. My wife was blissfully unaware of this routine. Later on, when she entered school, I stopped waking her up, but she knew that once I came back from office, I would spend some time in her room. I would go through her books, her school diary and things like that, so that I could connect with her at her level. Today she is 15, and I'm like her friend. She discusses 'math to males' (as I call it) with me.'

   I do not want to use the clichéd term 'quality time' as any time spent in the company of your child is quality time.

But the essential thing is to 'be with' your child and not just to 'be around' him. **Smsing your friends or checking emails while giving the child a mobile or a video game to play with does not count as time spent with him.** Most young parents have their babies at a time when they are also concentrating on their careers. Travelling over distances to reach work places, managing tough bosses, or rising to your own expectations can be very taxing. So where in the world is there any time at all to spend with your child?

You have to make time for that. Connecting with your child at a very young age ensures the linkages in the subconscious. Your child grows up knowing that you are a rock solid support for him when needed.

3. **Nurture**: The father's role as a nurturer helps both boys and girls. Boys grow confident of their masculinity and girls do not look out for premature romances and relationships. The image of a strong father in the background is very reassuring and hence they do not look outside.

Mahesh, 55, is a father of two grown up children. His son today works in a multinational and is expecting his own child soon. Says Mahesh, 'The only advice I give my son, Jatin, aged 27, is that he needs to nurture his child. Talking to them, playing with them, keeping peace when their minds are in turmoil is the best way a father can nurture his children. When Jatin was in school and had a showdown with his friends over a class programme, he was very upset. He raved and ranted about it for an entire week. All I did was listen to him. He found a confidant in me. He could crib to someone who wasn't judgemental about the entire situation. As I gave him a third person perspective on the situation, he could figure out the solutions for himself. This incident taught him to reflect, and today he is a stronger individual, capable of taking the right decisions with the right perspective.'

4. **Discipline**: The tendency of most fathers is to confuse discipline with anger. If your wife's favourite tactic with your child is: 'wait till daddy gets home', then you need to have a relook at your techniques for disciplining. If children begin to equate daddy's disciplining with anger, then rebellion is not too far away.

   Gautam, a father of a 7-year-old, recently told me about his encounter with his son. 'I was jolted out of my senses the day I saw Rutuj banging away at the table shouting "Why can't you listen to me? Is it so difficult to follow a simple thing?" I left my newspaper and ran over to him to ask him what happened. Rutuj was upset that the cat was not listening to what he said! "But why are you shouting like this?" I asked him. He yelled back at me, "When you do it to me, I listen na! From now on even I am not going to listen." That day I realized raising your voice and getting anger was leading me nowhere.'

5. **Protect and provide**: The father is historically and traditionally seen as a protector and provider. The role continues but in a changed manner. Research has consistently shown that fathers who are ably employed and are able to provide and protect have happy families. Fathers who are not, usually do not have meaningful relations within the family.

6. **Guide your child to the world outside**: Children realize role demarcations very early in life. Toddlers know who is going out of the house and usually cling on to that person.

Varsha, 24, a fashion designer says, 'My 8-month-old would know exactly when her grandpa gets dressed to leave home. She would tug at his trousers till he picked her up and took her out for a few minutes before he left for work.'

Children soon realize that fathers go out more than anyone else in the family. This makes them believe that the father knows more about what's outside the home. Use that to your benefit. Guide your child through his journey through life.

The more involved you are with them in their younger years, the more they will confide in you when they get older.

Talk to adolescents about the problems you envisage. Talk about drugs, alcohol, pre-marital unprotected sex, and other sensitive issues to your teenager. The bonding that happens during the teenage years lasts a lifetime. Once your child is convinced he has a friend at hand and not a preacher, he will not fear in confiding in you. Mingle with his/her friends. Children whose parents know most of their friends tend to develop stronger friendships in life.

7. **Be a positive role model:** Do what you want your children to do. If you ignore road signals, bribe policemen, use abusive language, and berate all and sundry expect your child to do the same. The qualities that you display will be the ones your children imbibe. If you have many friends, your child will imbibe the quality and have many friends too.

Acknowledge your mistakes. This is usually seen as a weakness but it is a positive quality. It helps children to know that while making mistakes is a part of life, accepting mistakes and the willingness to learn from them is more important.

Mahesh tells me about another incident with Ketan, his younger son, when he was around 15 years old. Ketan had a curfew of 10 pm for a party that he wanted to attend. But he came back only at 12 in the morning. 'Why are there rules only for me? Papa goes out and comes by 2 am after saying that he will be back by 11 pm. No one yells at him. So he can do what he wants.' I realized the truth in what he was saying and since then I too have maintained curfew times. Ketan fell into track and never again broke his curfew. Now he is past his curfew age but he makes it a point to let us know if he will be late. He knows that we worry about him.'

8. **Have a good relationship with the mother of the child**: Children who witness affectionate, caring, and loving behaviour by the father towards their mother usually instinctively realize that they can trust their father. Research shows that children who witness strong and happy marriages are usually strong and well rounded individuals themselves. In today's world of fragile marriages, holding on to a meaningless relationship at times can cause more harm than anything else.

Whether married or not, as a dad, maintain a respectful relation with the mother of your child. Your child values her and you should be able to give importance to that value. How the father behaves with the mother has different implications for the son and the daughter. Boys who see their fathers misbehave with their mothers grow up confused about the right way to behave with women in their adult life. As far as possible, handle your issues with the mother of your child constructively and peacefully. Girls who grow up seeing their father in an abusive relationship with their mother usually have tumultuous relationships in their own lives. They generally tend to distrust men.

How am I different to my son and my daughter?

This is a question that worries many fathers. Every father realizes that his son and daughter respond to him differently. This necessitates a difference in the way the father behaves with his son and daughter. The difference that nature has made inherent in the way a boy and a girl behave cannot be denied.

Father–son

Every father in India still believes that a son is a pathway to heaven and is his '*waaris*', the keeper of his lineage. The changing nature of this relationship is, however, now very visible in social settings. Sons and fathers today do seem to share a sort of friendship that did not exist earlier. Dr D. Charles Williams, a psychologist, has identified five predictable stages that can occur in the way that sons relate to their fathers throughout their lives with the acronym IDEAL.

- **Idolize:** This refers to our childhood view of our fathers, when they seem invincible.
- **Discord:** This occurs during the rebellious teen years, when we typically want to be nothing like our fathers.
- **Evolving:** During young adulthood, our difference or contempt turns into something more like competition.
- **Acceptance:** Occurs during our 30s and 40s when we let go of grudges and acknowledge our father's positive traits. Friendship often begins to evolve in this stage.
- **Legacy:** In our 50s, we will recognize that we are a living product of our fathers influence.[1]

The modern day father wants to be a friend to his son. At times you may find yourself oscillating between wanting to play the all powerful father and the totally hands-on father.

'My sons will be teenagers soon. I know there will be a stage when they will move out and have lives of their own. From young boys who looked up to me for sports and games, I noticed things changed when they began to sprout facial hair! They no longer wanted me to pet them or cuddle them. I began to talk to them, not at them. I spoke to them about the world of drugs, unprotected sex, and alcohol. This made a world of difference,' says Ashwin, 42, a computer programmer.

Father–daughter

A father is the first male that a girl encounters. This relationship usually decides how she handles her relationships with men later on in life. The identification of herself as a female is largely shaped by how her father accepts her.

'My father maintained a distance from me once I attained puberty. I was told by my mom not to sit next to him or touch him. When I went out with him, I would be careful not to hold his hand. This was scary as I was very close to my father before I started getting my periods. I was very confused. Why did things change just like that? I had no answer. Later on in school and college, I always believed that I had to keep my distance from boys. Even now I find it very intimidating to talk to men freely,' rues Lakshmy, a 35-year-old teacher rues. 'It took some time and effort on the part of my husband to turn me around from this insecurity. And today I find it so refreshing to see my daughter and husband share a camaraderie, which deep down I even envy,' she laughs.

Lakshmy's case is not isolated. Many societies in India do not encourage too much father–daughter interaction once the girl has attained puberty. However, most girls grow up idolizing their fathers and look for a father figure in their future partners.

It's important for daughters to know that dads respect their identity. Dads also need to convey to their daughters that it's safe to display their affection to them.

'Psychologist Dr Linda Nielsen has been studying the father–daughter relationship for over 15 years. Like researchers before her, she acknowledges that positive fathering produces well-adjusted, confident, and successful daughters who relate well to the men in their lives.'[2] Daughters need to know that the first man in their life loved them unconditionally. This relationship forms the basis of all further relationships in life, especially the romantic ones. According to Dr Nielson and many other researchers, the father–daughter relationship not only affects their further relationships, it also influences the onset of puberty in girls. Girls who have good relationships with their father reach puberty later than those who don't. Research has shown that when a girl is not getting the attention and affirmation she so desperately needs from her father, puberty is triggered prematurely in an unconscious attempt to attract the attention of other men instead. And early onset of menstruation is an established risk factor for breast cancer later in life, with each year of delay decreasing the risk by 10 to 20 percent.

Fathers can teach daughters to understand the limits of public behaviour. Research shows that fathers are able to provide daughters with unique perspectives, enhancing their understanding of men, providing opportunities to role play communication strategies with men. When the girl is confident in the presence of her father, she knows she can interact with any other male. A father teaches his daughter important lessons about negotiating with people. If the father is overtly critical, she will begin to believe all men are enemies. If he constantly criticizes the way she dresses or the way she speaks, the daughter will grow up to believe that all men think just like that and her opinions will get clouded by his perspectives. But if he is open to debate, then she will develop the confidence to present her own opinions. A father decides if his daughter turns out to be a submissive, an aggressive or an assertive individual. His interaction with her gives the male perspective to life, thus moulding her future interactions with other men.

Father	
With Son	With Daughter
Recognize that sons are influenced by their fathers. Your behaviour will determine your son's behaviour.	Respect her mom. The way you treat her mom will make her respect you.
Develop common interests. You and your son may not share all the same hobbies. Find one or two common spaces. Spend time with each other.	Get to know her interests. Go to her matches, paint along with her, listen to her practise the piano.
Indulge in boisterous play. Play safe even when you play rough. Boys love action and it doesn't hurt to play boisterously with them.	Take her out for a movie or lunch; only the two of you. You will really bond with her.
Take on a big project—painting your car, volunteering in camps; something that fascinates your son.	Get to know her friends, especially once you know she is old enough for girl talk. Call them for sleep overs.

Father	
With Son	**With Daughter**
Be confident of your upbringing and let your son realize his life in the fullest manner. Effective communication is the key. Listen to them before you talk to them.	Listen, listen, listen! Girls just want to be heard.
Talk about sex and relationships.	Be there at every milestone; her first class party, her first stage performance, her first date, her efforts to get into college.
Focus on the positives. Create ways to celebrate their achievements.	Keep the promises you make. Girls value promises and commitment.
Give enough time to each child. Spend time separately with each one too.	Spend time on school work too. It lets her know you care.
Help your son gain his spiritual ground. Talk to him about faith, religion, God, nature, etc.	Hug her, give her the good night kisses. They need to be shown you love them, not just told.

Who is a mother?

A Hindu Shloka says 'Mata Pita Guru Daivom', which means 'Mother Father Teacher God'. But at a subconscious level, it reinstates the position of the mother in a child's life—first and foremost. The child knows the mother from the time of conception to birth; it's the mother who nurtures her. Through the mother the child knows the father, the teacher, and finally God. A mother is born when a child is born.

The role of the mother too has undergone significant transformation. From being home bound and caring for the needs of the family, a mother today has to balance the world of work and home. She now is a person who has an identity independent of the family, yet is the one person who keeps the family together.

I am a mother but what makes me a mom?

The answer to this is not going to be very different from what it is for a father. The expectations from a mother vis a vis a father as far as parenting goes are similar. The difference is in the levels of involvement. If the shloka places the mother before the father, it is because the mother's influence on the child has far more reaching effects on the subconscious of the child.

Pre-natal bonding

The mother–child bond begins as early as five months into the foetal stage. The baby begins to recognize the mother's voice. Talk to your baby. Sing to her. Get the other siblings and the father to talk to her. Babies develop a sense of warmth and security. I will discuss this at length later in the book.

Just after birth

Traditionally women went to their parents houses for their deliveries and stayed there till the baby was at least 3 months old. This is the most crucial period in a child's life. The child identifies the mother within minutes of birth. The bonding that happens in the initial stages of the child's life is very important. During the initial stages, the mother lives with the child almost 24×7. She bathes, feeds, cuddles, plays, and soothes the baby. The bonding that develops at that time lasts a lifetime. The child develops a feeling of security with the mother.

Through various stages of life

As your child climbs each step, the way you influence your child will keep changing. As a toddler, she will look up to you for comfort, food, and love. As a young girl she will look up to you for worldly wisdom and guidance. As a teenager she will need you as a friend. A young boy too will look upon the mother as his pillar of strength.

From the maids to the local vegetable vendor, children see their mothers interacting with a whole host of people. The way you behave with the different people who play different roles in their lives, will shape how children behave with them in later stages. Talk to them about how they perceive these people, answer their questions and concerns about cultures and traditions.

Radha, 25, is a working woman. She has two children. She celebrates all the festivals and functions at home. If it's Christmas they have a Christmas tree and Santa. If it's Diwali, they light up their house with candles and make sweets. They play dandiya and also share sweets on Eid. Radha says, 'Living in a cosmopolitan society, I encourage my children to participate in all festivals. Not only are they culturally more aware, they are growing to be global citizens. If they cannot embrace their neighbour, how will they embrace other cultures when they travel around the world tomorrow?'

This cultural extravaganza in our country is a heritage that our children can imbibe.

How am I different to my daughter and my son?

Mother–daughter

I recently came across this little card on Facebook, which sums up the mother–daughter relationship beautifully.

At 6 years:	'Mommy, I love you.'
At 10 years:	'Mom, whatever.'
At 16 years:	'My mom is so annoying!'
At 18 years:	'I wanna leave this house!'
At 25 years:	'Mom, you were right.'
At 30 years:	'I want to go to mom's house.'
At 50 years:	'I don't want to lose my mom.'
At 70 years:	'I would give up everything for my mom to be here with me.'

A mother–daughter relationship is a complex one. Recent studies show that female children are most affected by their mothers. 'In fact, things like body image, attitudes about men, trusting people, dreams, and success are often facilitated (or thwarted) by this relationship. A daughter who feels empowered by her mother, will feel empowered in life. A daughter who does not feel accepted by her mother will never feel accepted by anyone else (or herself).'[3]

Every daughter has had one fight (at the very least) with her mother. From being the centre of the daughter's world you will soon find yourself at loggerheads with her over everything—clothes, make up, friends, food. Daughters look at mothers with two very contrasting points of view. A mother can be both friend and foe. They are of the same gender and hence girls instinctively feel they can trust them, and it is for this very reason that the mother also becomes a foe. The mother vies for attention and love of the father. The daughter sees the mother as a threat to her affection towards her father. So as a mom to your little girl, tread gently.

Revathi, 32, a teacher says, 'I remember interacting more with my mum during my teenage years. She was not only very strict about my academic performance but also about the clothes I wore. She ensured that I attended all the required classes—music, dance, etc. She was like Amy Chua, the tiger mother. But I soon disconnected with her. I did things so that she wouldn't nag me. I never found any meaning in those activities. The music classes remain a painful testimony to my growing up years. The minute I finished school I joined a college where I had to stay in a hostel, only to be away from her and enjoy the freedom. Today I am more at peace with her. Being a mother, I look at her from a different perspective. But yes, I do feel bad about the fact that it took us so many years to get on the same page.'

A widely held belief is that a daughter grows up to resemble her mother. Freud established the theory of same sex similarity between parents and children. This theory was later modified by Nancy Chodorow, a feminist sociologist and psychoanalyst. She brought in the theory that both boys and girls have a special bond with the mother as they grow up. Boys subsequently have to find a role for themselves unlike their mother while girls find it easier to follow the role model in front of them.

While mothering a daughter, try to refrain from reliving your life through her. During her teen years remember that she is trying to discover her own identity. Let her be. Do not impose yourself on her. She will soon realize that the friend she is searching for has been with her the whole time. Give her the sense of security to discuss everything. Do not make topics taboo or she will shy away from discussing issues such as boyfriends, sex, and contraception with you. She is losing out on a lot of learning due to your stiff upper lip! Girls place a lot of importance on relationships. Nurture that.

Mother–son

The mother–son relationship in India is almost a venerated one. It is the most spoken about and the most represented one in our mythology and culture. Who can forget Shashi Kapoor's famous dialogue—'Mere paas maa hai'? The mother of a son has always garnered more respect in our society. The mother–son relationship is equally complicated. A boy will grow up to become a man, but a mother will continue to remain a mother. Indian society has many instances of 'mama's boys'. Boys are mollycoddled by their mothers and pampered to the extent of making them dependant on the mother for everything. The son becomes the reason for the mother's existence. Even today, in many places the lady is called by her own husband as the mother of their child, for example, 'Ramu ki maa'. There are many cases when boys are not able to cut off the umbilical cord even after getting married. Just as fathers need to draw a line with the physical intimacy with their daughters, mothers need to a draw line with their sons.

'As a child, Raj Kapoor often bathed with his beautiful mother and said that 'seeing her nude left a deep erotic impression on my mind'. And that no doubt inspired his sensual celluloid heroines in wet, see-through saris.'[4]

For a boy, his mother is his first interaction with the female kind. She invariably becomes a role model while choosing a future mate. Hence, your responsibility towards your son is magnified. Your actions today will have a reaction in the later days of the child. D.H. Lawrence, in his novel, *Sons and Lovers*, brings out how a mother can hold her son's soul with her. Mrs Morell's sons are never able to cut off the umbilical cord and as a result are unable to have fulfilling relationships with any girl. Her imprint lies so strong on their psyche that they never have a fulfilling relationship with any partner. 'The primitive desire for the one parent may also awaken in the child a jealous motivation to exclude the other parent. A critical point of awakening is where the child realizes that the mother has affections for others besides him.'[5] This may cause the child to cling to the mother.

Indian mothers are known to pamper their sons so much that even as adults they begin to look for their mothers in their wives. Most Indian women will tell you that 'the other woman' in their lives is usually not the husband's girlfriend but his mother.

As your son grows up, you have to understand that he is no longer a boy. His raging hormones make him a man. But if you continue to treat him as a baby and 'mother' him, he begins to unconsciously get sexual gratification from that. This stops him from looking out of the family for this fulfilment. These instances are stronger when the mother is single.

Thirty-year-old Leela is married to Harish. They have a 5-year-old son. Her only issue with Harish is that he can't see beyond his mother. Leela experiences great frustration at times. 'Even for small things like pre-school admission for our son, he tells me that he will admit him only if Ba (his mother) allows it. I'm not a part of any of the decisions! If I want to send him to a summer camp, Ba needs to sanction it. Harish argues that it was her decisions regarding him that helped him achieve success, so why should he not use that same expertise? I see his dependency on his mother and his unwillingness to come out of the sheltered cocoon. He is always the child,' she rues.

A mother is threatened by the presence of another woman in her son's life. 'A mother's bitter, angry, or resentful attitude is equally as damaging to a son's sense of self-esteem and will ultimately have an effect on his relationships with other women. Mothers who hold on to negative attitudes about men are inadvertently projecting these attitudes on their sons. Boys think that their mothers feel the same way about them as they do about other men and go to great lengths to counter any negativity for fear of losing the maternal love that they cherish.'[6]

Mothers	
With Son	With Daughter
Teach him that honesty is the most important thing in a relationship.	Show your daughter you are proud to be a woman.
Teach him to learn to take 'no' for an answer. Other people have a right to say 'no' and that's not an insult to his manhood.	Spend as much time with your daughter as you would with your son. Help her discover what she likes to do, wants to try, and doesn't like to do.
Don't assume that he does things because he is a boy. His actions are encouraged by your words or by your silence.	Focus on her strengths. Help her go through adolescence with a strong self image.
Teach him to treat a girl well. Teach him to respect a woman.	Motivate her to be assertive. Teach her how to pave her own path.
Forget gender roles. Avoid stereotyping him.	Be open minded about her career choices. Do not let her gender limit her dreams.

Gene N. Landrum in his book *Entrepreneurial Genius, the Power of Passion* has given examples of how fathers have influenced daughters, and mothers their sons. He says 'The greatest imprinting influence came, most often, from the parent of the opposite gender. Groomed by a fearless mother, Richard Branson grew into an untamed business icon. Eve Branson, a flight attendant when flying was more for thrill than transportation, spent many hours grooming her first born to live on the edge. He rose to meet her challenges and succeeded beyond her wildest expectations as a flamboyant risk taking entrepreneur. Martha Stewart dedicated her first book to her father. He was her mentor, her friend, confidant, and role model for perfection.'

At home we have the very famous father–daughter politicians who changed the history of this country: Pandit Jawaharlal Nehru and Indira Gandhi. Nehru's influence on Indira is well known and commented on.

The influence of the parent on the progeny is eternal. A positive influence on your children will lead to success in their lives.

The dark side of gender stereotypes

Gender stereotyping has its own pitfalls. It puts people into typical brackets that forces people to behave because of their gender. Some typical gender stereotypes are:

Girls: are weak both physically and emotionally. They cannot handle criticism. They need to learn only how to look after their families. There is no need for them to be educated enough to work out of home. They are emotional and lack the practical skills to handle situations. They are moody and this affects their working.

Boys: are physically and emotionally strong, to the extent of being able to be cold and insensitive. Boys have to look after families and hence need to work out of home. They are more practical and take logical decisions. They are not affected by moods.

The fact that such stereotypes exist create many prejudices. These are assumptions which disregard a person's abilities in favour of general trends. Choices and options get limited due to this. Girls are not presented with options of taking up careers which require heavy physical work because of such attitudes.

Through history it has been noticed that women have been paid less even when they did the same type of jobs as men. This was only because of the belief that women need not be paid as much only because they were women. The case of Razia Sultan who was a strong administrator but failed to make it as the ruler of Delhi is classic. The nobility refused to support her as her abilities were clouded by the fact that she was a woman.

Gender stereotyping affects not only women. Men come under tremendous pressure to play their masculine roles. A man is supposed to be macho, protective, and earn the bread for his home and look after the family. A sensitive man is often teased as being effeminate or weak. Men are portrayed in most media as violent, sexually abusive, and incompetent fathers. We often tell kids to be aware of men rather than women.

Be wary of reinforcing these stereotypes on your children.

Boys are from Mars, Girls are from Venus

My son and daughter tell me where they are in very different ways. I know where my son is because I hear him. I know where my daughter is because she tells me.

Anonymous

Most people struggling through a relationship have read *Men are from Mars and Women are from Venus* to work through their woes and their frustrations of having to deal with the opposite sex. The fact is that while we fight tooth and nail for equality of the sexes, we are essentially different.

There are fundamental differences in the brain structures of boys and girls that parents should be aware. I recently spoke at a women's leadership conference on the fundamental difference of the two brains and how it affects leadership styles and why women are now increasingly being looked at for key leadership positions. I spoke about how men tend to be more task oriented, women more relationship oriented. Men tend to be more autocratic and transactional, women more democratic. Men more directive, while women participative and transformational. An article in *Business Week* stated that: 'After years of analyzing what makes leaders most effective and figuring out who's got the Right Stuff, management gurus now know how to boost the odds of getting a great executive: Hire a female.'

A page from a mother's diary

'You know, Mamma, then Bubbles caught the frog and put it inside his socks. Then he took it up to our classroom and placed it on the floor beside his desk. By the time Miss Prerna entered the class, the frog was jumping around and croaking. The boys clapped, hooted, and the girls screamed and huddled in one corner. Miss was very angry and wrote in Bubbles' diary that she wants to meet you tomorrow after school. Bubbles, GO—show Mamma your diary.'

My 12-year-old daughter, Bunny's eyes shone in anticipation of my reaction after her well-animated commentary. She was obviously expecting some high drama from my end.

I looked at him. He neither budged, nor moved, nor uttered a word of protest throughout his sister's report on his not-so-savoury deeds in school. There stood my 12-year-old—a portion of his crushed and dirty shirt hanging outside his shorts, hair dishevelled, head hung down, standing still, staring at his finger nails. I drew him close to me and asked, 'Why have you done this, son? Wasn't it just a week back that you brought that kitten home and hid it in your cupboard? I explained to you why it wasn't the right thing to do, didn't I? Why have you done it again?'

'M-A-M-M-A!!' Bunny interrupted as usual. 'I thought you'd give him a good dressing down for this! But you aren't scolding him at all. You're s-o-o-o partial! If I eat the whole packet of Oreo biscuits after lunch then that is wrong, but when Bubbles carries a frog to class, you don't scold him at all, WHY? I know you love him more than me, I know for sure.' And the predictable happened—she burst into tears, ran to her room, and slammed the door shut.

I turned towards him. He quietly said, 'I wanted to bring the frog home because I wanted to keep it as a pet. Mamma, will Miss Prerna shout at you tomorrow?'

'Even if she does, will you feel bad for me?' I asked.

'I don't know. I'm hungry, gimme lunch.'

Matter closed. I often wonder why it is so difficult for me to talk to my boy. Any question relating to 'how do you feel' or 'what do you think' has been routinely resisted by his 'I don't know' or 'I don't understand these things'. But before you can even ask my girl anything to the same effect, she is ready with a whole list of answers—how she feels and why and what she feels, why/what/how her brother should feel, or I and her father should feel!

How children change with time! When Bubbles and Bunny were toddlers, Bubbles was the one who would howl and cry to express his likes/dislikes and Bunny would be my quiet angel playing all by herself. But now, they seem to have swapped places. I wonder—are all boys different from girls in terms of their behaviour and attitudes or am I stereotyping them? Whatever it is, I have begun to feel that raising a boy child is not exactly the same as raising a girl child. They look at life differently and expect parents to treat them differently, too.'

For any one of us who has had a relationship with the opposite sex, we know that men and women are very different creatures indeed and this difference kicks in from childhood. We reinforce it, of course. I know a father who picks his son up whenever he falls, rubs his knee and says, 'Brave boy. You did not cry. Go play.' The same father, when his daughter falls, reacts by hitting the ground where she fell, saying, 'Naughty floor. You hurt my baby!'

How is a boy child different from a girl child?

'Raj and I child-proofed our entire apartment when Nidhi began to crawl. We thought we were ready for everything until Nevaan came along three years ago. He climbs on everything and throws everything out of the window—the table clock, hair brush, books, the newspaper. His latest fascination is to hang from my open kitchen cabinet door. I'm constantly worried that he's either going to hurt himself or trash the house. How can my kids be so different? They are both being raised in the same environment.' Rashmi narrated to me one evening over a cup of tea. 'So, how then will the parenting techniques you tell me about have the same impact on both of them when boys and girls are so different right from the beginning? Do you think the same methods will work?'

To answer the question let us look at the difference between boys and girls.

For all the equality that the genders may claim in social life, the fact remains that girls and boys are different.

In the last two decades we have learnt so much about the difference in male and female brain structures, yet we educate and parent boys and girls in the same way. Without going into the science at great length, the major differences that exist due to differing brain structures are that:

- in most cases, female brains mature earlier than male brains;
- females can acquire complex verbal skills including reading, achieving a larger vocabulary, and mastering grammar much earlier than males. This makes males rely heavily on non-verbal communication and are less likely to verbalize feelings. Current research also suggests that 67 percent of males throughout their life are visual learners. This means that they do not benefit from learning that relies on conversation and words;
- the corpus callosum in the brain is a bundle of nerves that connects emotion and cognition. In females it is up to 20 percent larger than in males, which is why females are usually better at making decisions and anything else requiring sensory processing skills. This means that females have better verbal abilities and research suggests that this is a major reason why women are also better at multi-tasking;
- brain chemicals in males and females differ. The male brain secretes less serotonin than in the female, making the male more impulsive in general; and

- females release higher levels of oxtocin, which makes them capable of quicker and more immediate empathetic responses to others' pain and needs. Oxtocin also reduces the amount of cortisol, the stress hormone, and facilitates bonding. It may be called the 'cuddle hormone' in this respect because it tends to encourage more affection. Thus, females are better at expressing their emotions.

Apart from the differences in the brain, we also know that there are essential hormonal differences between males and females. Females are dominated by estrogen and progesterone. Males by testosterone. Simply put, men usually require more action. There are a lot of subtle learning differences because of this but I will include those in a teaching guide! From a parenting point of views we need to be aware that boys will speak fewer words than girl, and will probably start talking later than the girl. The boy child will need more movement, even when studying, as this helps them to stimulate their brains and relieve impulsive behaviour. Boys and girls both like pictures and visual diagrams but boys will rely on them more than girls.

We as parents naturally need to be discreet while making decisions on what will work the best for our children. Our daily interaction with and observation of our child makes us more knowledgeable than any educator or psychologist to identify the uniqueness in him.

These evolutionary differences notwithstanding, the general level of intelligence in boys and girls is similar. Leonard Sax, the author of *Why Gender Matters,* says, 'There are no differences in *what* girls and boys can learn. But there are big differences in *the way* to teach them.'

Why?

Raising a boy child is not the same as raising a girl child

As anatomical differences make genders, differences in brain chemistry make sexes. It is a proven truth that sex differences are real and not just stereotypical brouhaha. To a great extent it determines one's views, judgement, behaviour, and attitude towards life. Therefore, it is necessary on our part to raise our sons differently than our daughters because their needs and demands are sexually different. Although the differences do not apply to all boys and girls, they apply to most, and their effects on parenting can prove to be useful knowledge.

How to deal differently with boys and girls

Communicate with boys through action and girls through talking

Most mothers claim that communication with their boys, especially teens and above, has been their toughest challenge. Even Bubbles and Bunny's mother complained about it. **Boys respect action. So act more and talk less with them.**

If you say you're going to give your son a whole bar of Bournville chocolate and then you don't, you will lose your credibility. If you say that you will lend him your Smartphone to take to college and then back out, he will lose his faith in you. If you explain the situation to a girl, she will usually understand. But boys respect action more than words and when you don't follow through what you have promised him, it is like you haven't done much. As a result you may be ignored or dismissed. Even from an adult perspective, men feel unloved and disrespected if they do not get enough concrete evidence from their partner that they are valued more than anyone else. Therefore, not only in parental relationships, but in any relationship with men, act more and talk less. You will be trusted and respected.

With girls, however, it works differently. Just tell them you are angry and stop talking till they can behave better (not advocating that it is the correct thing to do!), they will think over the consequences and come round. Why? Because they are anxious to maintain the relationship and will go a great length to maintain the status quo. They might try to use their superior verbal skills to defend themselves, argue their point, try to blame others, but in the end if you stick to your guns, they generally comply because the relationship itself is very important to them.

What is the justification for this approach?

Girls respond to verbal approach by talking things out. Therefore, talking could be an appropriate parenting style for girls. Boys require a different approach because they not only learn to talk later than girls and use more limited vocabularies, but they also have more trouble expressing their emotions in words. Take the case of Bubbles for instance, he did feel bad that his mother would get into trouble for his misdeeds, but he couldn't arrange his thoughts into words. All he could say was, 'I don't know. Gimme lunch.' (Perhaps that is why many of my psychotherapist friends claim that there is a much higher number of boys who visit their clinic. Their emotions pile up to a point where they require purging.) Since men do more and speak less, they are more involved in the action of life. They love action packed activities—roughing up, tumbling, and wrestling (usually at all ages). Most Shin Chan cartoons are a hit with all age groups—from 4 to 54—because Shin Chan Nohara is a precocious little 5-year-old, who often drives his mum and dad up the wall, drops his pants, bares his backside, and does a little jig if scolded. Boys make sounds associated with action—such as Vroom! Vroom!—while pulling their toy truck or cars. They do not watch your facial expression as much as they watch your actions.

For your boy child

When your boy reaches the age of 14, explain to him the importance of mastering people skills. Being only action-oriented won't do. So help him in studying faces intently and consciously read other non-verbal signals such as tone of voice while communicating with others. Tell him that words are like coins—they have another side to them, which must be read too. Close observation and experience exposes that side. Teach him the art of reading between the lines even when he is talking to someone over the phone or chatting or reading e-mails and SMSes. Teach him to be people-oriented.

For your girl child

When your girl is around 8 years of age, teach her not to be so overly concerned about other's opinions because not all criticism (from so-called elders) is well-meaning. This is a tactic many people adopt. Since girls are adept at communicating, they give undue importance to what others say. Bunny was upset that Mamma did not scold Bubbles hard enough but was always angry with her.

Start to establish an open communication with your daughter once she is 8 or 9, so that she can come to you any time for advice to know what criticism is well-meaning and what is not, so that she learns whom to take seriously and who not to. As she grows up, encourage her to confide and seek advice from a trusted mentor or a very trusted friend.

A girl's hearing is more sensitive and the verbal centres in their brain develop more quickly than in a boy. When it comes to warning or reprimanding her, remember how sensitive she is about her image, so never admonish her publicly.

Disciplining boys and girls

Disciplining is essential for how a child turns out. Just as much as food is essential for the body, discipline is essential to train the mind. The methods of disciplining a child are what make all the difference. Disciplining leads to the ability to work well with peers. It also fosters the ability to think not just about oneself, but also the society at large. Disciplining your child is not about creating conflict. It is about empowering him with the skills to make the right decisions at the right time and right place.

There are three types of learners—visual, auditory, and kinesthetic. **Visual learners** respond well to visual inputs and stimuli. They are the children who can 'read' McDonalds and Coca-Cola before they have been taught the alphabet!

Auditory learners can follow instructions and tend to lean a lot on their auditory input. These children can recite jingles from television commercials after hearing them only a few times.

Kinesthetic learners require movement to learn. These children need to physically manipulate things like base ten blocks to conceptually understand numbers.

These learning styles not only impact how you will teach your child but also the way children can be taught discipline. Visual learners pick up many visual clues. So if you put your fingers on your lips, they get the message to be quiet. Kinesthetic learners need to be held, cuddled, and possibly shown how they need to behave. Auditory learners will benefit if you say 'Shhhh'. What does not work is if you yell 'quiet!' to a kinesthetic child.

For your boy child

'Finish your studies and I will give you my iPad to play games on.'

Discipline a boy child mainly with a reward because they don't respond to verbal approach. In the book, *The Minds of Boys: Saving Our Sons from Falling Behind in School and Life,* researchers Michael Gurian and co-author Kathy Stevens say that the brain of the boy is different from the girl. Boys tend to be more kinesthetic, spatial, mechanic, and hands-on learners. They rely a lot on their gross motor skills. (To mention in passing, boys are more impulsive particularly as toddlers and when they are in their pre-primary years. Experts say these developmental differences contribute to the mislabeling of their normal behaviour as problematic.) The mother who has observed them either fighting or turning every activity into a contest will agree. Parents need to be more patient and lenient with them at this developmental stage.

What is the justification behind this reward system?

Many parents tell me that the system of rewards is like 'bribery'. Then I tell them, 'Do you feel getting paid by your employer is bribery? Why do you then work for money? Only because the money is needed to run your home or because you feel your effort is getting its due respect?'

Reward is encouraging and we work hard for it because it tangibly acknowledges our efforts. So we cannot really complain if a similar system works well for our children. The world of action is rich with meaning and the examples are too numerous to mention here. Reward them for good deeds done. It's not bribery.

How to reward?

Boys are natural risk-takers—encourage them

In their growing up years, and until they are well into their teens, it will be difficult for you to keep your house in order because your boys will turn it into an indoor sports centre. Your dining table will turn into a TT table, the passage from the hall to your bedroom their cricket pitch, and the whole house their football ground. Even their father will join in their activities for old times' sake. What can you do? Precious little indeed.

Encourage them to slow down a little (chances are they won't listen). It is, after all, their male hormone, testosterone, speaking. They will be a little aggressive compared to girls. So you will have to learn to tolerate the behaviour or be prepared to be frustrated. But this too shall pass. Only the empty nest with its cracked glasses and damaged music system will stand as mute mementoes of their growing up years.

Experts say taking risks lights up the pleasure centres of their brains. That is why most parents say they have to keep a closer eye on what a son is 'getting into', or use more bandages, or keep the orthopaedic's cell number handy until they are at least out of school. But letting kids explore—at the cost of a few scrapes and cuts—helps build their character, self-confidence, resilience, and self-reliance. Let them take risks. Somewhere down the line it'll be of use when they have to take strategic decisions at the spur of the moment and will have no one to turn to.

For your girl child

Girls are apprehensive—persuade them to take more risks

Girls generally take safe risks or no risks at all. That is why you need to look for opportunities for your daughter to jump off a wall, swim in the deep end, or try the bigger slide till she is in her tweens. Encourage her to take more risks and push the horizon further. Later on they will be glad they did.

Girls focus more on feelings. They are auditory learners. So if you speak to them about how you want them to behave and are able to attach an emotion to the behaviour you will find that they respond faster. If you tell your girl, 'Sheela will be happy if you played along with her, instead of pushing her away', you will find her reacting to this better than if you tell her, 'Why can't you just play with Sheela?' Whereas with your boy you may say, 'Imagine how much fun it will be when Tony and you play together! Which of your toys can he play with?'

Constructive criticism helps girls. They are more aware of what people think of them. Hence, do not reprimand them in public. Speak to her in private if you feel she has done something wrong.

Give them a choice between tasks like clearing the dinner table or doing the beds. This gives them the power to choose.

Research has proven that boys and girls have different bio-behavioural responses to risk-taking, which are to some extent due to the underlying hormonal differences between the two sexes. Boys take risks to move towards a danger to explore it, which is called fight response. It gives them a thrill. Alternatively they run away, which is their flight response. Girls are more likely to turn to others for support to defend themselves from perceived threats. They are generally guided by the 'tend-and-befriend' response. The 'tend and befriend' response is a woman's (or a girl's) way of responding to stress. It has been observed that under stress, women don't usually run away from situations. They try to tackle them by talking it out with their sisters or other women who have gone through similar situations.

Remember, the brain develops at different sequences in girls and boys. In their early years (before 6), most boys lag behind girls in developing attentiveness, self-control, language, and other fine motor skills like handwriting or drawing. But then again, boys are also four years ahead in mathematical skills than girls. Moreover, boys may be more of a handful early on but girls can be more challenging in the pre-teen years, crying or arguing at every given opportunity. So don't judge boys as less or more smart than girls too early. A successful parent is one who is available for both his son or daughter, participating in their growth. And as a parent you continue to play the roles of the coach, referee, and cheerleader. When they bloom to their fullest potentiality one day, you and I will have the last laugh.

If your children frequently cry that you are being unfair, you ought to examine how you are dealing with them. Did Bunny complain against Mamma being partial towards Bubbles because girls are better at recognizing such emotions? Could be; then again, perspectives vary. The fact is equal treatment among siblings is an important goal to strive for and our target is to raise good human beings who may not be stereotypically boys or girls. The fact is that while we talk about gender equality we know that the development of the brain in boys and girls is different and we can use that to our advantage when it comes to disciplining them.

The way forward

Greater exposure to information about bio-behavioural differences acting upon their learning and development patterns give the parents of today an advantage. Knowing the brain differences can help us bring up the performance of math in girls. For example, we know that a girl's learning style is more cooperatively based and, therefore, does not work well in the independent, non-collaborative thinking way math is learnt in most classrooms. Knowing that girls depend on language, teachers could incorporate reading and music into math lessons (or incorporate math into reading and music lessons for boys). Empirical research in this area has proved that while the math achievement gap or language achievement gap is caused by the difference in the boy/girl brain, what it also shows is that girls actually do better in math and boys in language in those schools that practice the greatest degree of gender equality and look at working with the brain differences for greater achievement. Moreover, research has also proven that gender-neutral parenting, meaning making both the boy and girl practice more in their weak areas—boys practising more of creative writing and girls more math—can bring about all round development in both. In this way you can ensure equitable development, at least, where education is concerned.

Math vs language: Encourage your daughter to be academically competitive in everything from English, science, and math. There is no reason for girls to not excel in what have been considered till date as 'male' subjects; make sure she knows that as a parent you believe in her capabilities.

Tell your son that he needs to switch off the TV or laptop and read books. You may be faced with shrugs and grunts but encourage them to speak to you. Initiate dialogues.

Spatial skills (ability to locate objects in three dimensional space using sight or touch) **vs nurturing skills:** Playing sports, chess, block play, or building games can help girls improve spatial abilities. Finding one's way to a destination following landmarks or driving, can help in promoting spatial abilities.

To foster nurturing skills in boys, they should be encouraged to engage in caregiving activities like babysitting, tutoring younger siblings, or spending time with their grandparents.

Gender bias at home

Father's have a general tendency to be more protective of their daughters and mother's more permissive to sons (this is psychologically proven). But that should not be an alibi for the following common family trends.

1. Do not make girls learn housework more than boys on the grounds that they have to take charge of the household later in life. When they turn 18 and leave the home for higher studies and later for outstation job postings, both need these skills to set up a household. Equal opportunity to learn cooking, chopping, shopping, washing, cleaning, dusting and other domestic tasks must be ensured. Therefore, do not send the message to girls that the

home is a woman's domain, and teach boys a 'learned helplessness'.

2. Boys often get to use the family car more than girls, thus granting them greater independence. Instead, leave the family car to both once they have a driving license.

3. Boys are given permission to take up an outstation job at an earlier age than daughters, thus providing them with earlier independence. Though there can be real safety issues that dictate parental decisions, such as which part of the country or world they will be stationed in, try as often as possible to make the same decisions for both your son and daughter.

Ensure equitable development where education is concerned and for that matter send them to the right kind of school. At home, break stereotypes that a boy always needs to be tough and a girl always needs to be pleasing. Rather, work to raise good human beings who think and behave sensibly. Perhaps, this is the best that we can do to help them build their personality and self-esteem.

The differences that nature has endowed girls and boys will reinforce stereotypes if we are indifferent to this as parents. And this is where subconscious programming plays a major role.

This reminds me of an incident which led to us changing a school policy in my organization. One day, 10-year-old Armaan, a student from one of my schools, walked into my office to ask me a question. 'Ms Lina, why can't boys have long hair? When you regularly talk to us about the need to avoid gender stereotyping, why does the school diary say that boys need to have their hair cropped? If the only thing we need to ensure is that hair shouldn't fall into our eyes, we too can wear hair bands, can't we?'

This got me thinking, and I realized the simplicity and truth in the little boy's argument. Historically, we have a tradition of men sporting long hair. So why not today? I soon had a

---

Simple Parenting Actions to Avoid Stereotyping Your Children

- Cuddle your son, paint with him, and sing with him.
- Play video games with your girl.
- Encourage them to care for their grandparents.
- Both need to learn to set the dinner table and clear up later.
- Avoid statements like: 'It's okay for him to do that, he is a boy', 'You can't do this, you are a girl.'
- Aggression is a negative trait in both boys and girls. Do not encourage it or ignore it.
- Encourage your boy child especially to find 'words' for his feelings.
- Praise a boy who serves lunch to his grandmom as much as a girl who stands up against a rude auto driver. Encourage every form of positive social behaviour.
- Boys respect action. If you have promised something, keep your word or else he will lose faith in you.
- Girls respect thought. If you discuss a problem with your girl, she feels involved.
- If your son cries after a fall or gets hurt, understand his pain. Don't try to toughen him up.
- If you daughter likes karate more than dancing, encourage her. She doesn't have to conform to the 'girl' stereotype.
- At the same time, let kids be. If sonny boy wants to stick to his trucks and guns or the little lady at home is content being a princess, let them be. Avoid change for the sake of change.

meeting with my core team and changed the rule in our diaries. Today, boys in Billabong High can grow their hair as long as they want to as long as they maintain it neatly.

If you ever track down women who have excelled in some of the uncommon careers like sports or business, media or event management you will realize that the way up was not easy for them. They have had to fight very strong stereotypes before they actually reached where they are today. As a bahu I was supported and encouraged to be a teacher and even start my first pre-school. However, I recall a time when my 'hobby' turned into a full fledged business my in-laws actually sat my parents down to express their dissatisfaction and anxiety over what my business focus would do to my perceived primary focus—the family. Being a teacher is seen as a very noble and conventional career option for a woman, however, being a businesswoman is not as easily accepted.

If we encourage natural stereotypes and do not motivate girls to take risks or boys to empathize because we believe nature programmed them to do so, we risk parenting clones of what existed over the years. Let kids grow with their natural instincts, but motivate them to do different things. Break mindsets and work around stereotypes, foster a strong subconscious programme that will develop a strong self image in your children to handle the 21st century confidently.

The Early Years

I came out of the womb born to sing and dance. I have to follow my heart.

Jennifer Ellison

In the Mahabharata a pregnant Subhadra sat beside Arjun as he discussed the art of archery and war with Krishna. It is said that by hearing his father speak on the subject, Abhimanyu mastered the techniques of archery and war while still in the womb.

The story may be part of our mythology now, but it is not because of lack of scientific facts. Rick Gilmore, an associate professor of Psychology at Penn State, points to a well-known study conducted by Anthony DeCasper at the University of South Carolina. Gilmore says, 'There's ample evidence that foetuses are picking up information from the outside world. They're especially receptive to sounds from the mother's body and the external environment.'

According to Gilmore, that seems to prove the existence of pre-natal learning. 'Mothers were instructed to read Dr Seuss out loud while they were pregnant,' he explains. 'When the babies were born, researchers tested to see if they recognized Dr Seuss against other stories, and their mother's voice against other readers. In both cases, the infants were able to pick up on the vocal patterns they'd become familiar with in uterus.'

While we all agree that the first few years of the child are critical for his cognitive and physical development, it's also essential that the pre-natal months are emotionally well spent. We might feel that the baby will not understand anything, after all it's only a mass of cells, but the subconscious bank of the foetus begins to develop from the time of its inception. In *Magical Beginnings, Enchanted Lives*, Deepak Chopra explains what pregnancy research is indicating—'When a pregnant mother is anxious, stressed, or in a fearful state, the stress hormones released into her bloodstream cross through the placenta to the baby.'

Negative thoughts are often the root cause of a fear-based stress response. Deepak Chopra states, 'Stress activates the unborn child's endocrine system and influences foetal brain development. Children born to mothers who had intensely stressful pregnancies are more likely to have behavioural problems later in life. But when you feel joyful, your body produces natural pleasure chemicals called endorphins and encephalin. Stress free, your baby's nervous system works smoothly.'

Neeta, 25, became pregnant soon after her arranged marriage. She did not feel settled and was constantly in disagreements with her husband and her mother-in-law. Her parents lived in London. She was a stay-at-home mom. All the people she knew were her husband's friends and relatives as she was yet to make her friends in her new surroundings. She felt isolated and scared. When her baby was finally born, she was even more terrified. He cried most of the time, especially if he was not being held.

This case study is important in the light of new scientific findings. Dr Bruce Lipton, a stem cell biologist and bestselling author of *The Biology of Belief*, has formulated the theory of epigenetics. In this he says, 'The first eight weeks are the embryo phase where it is just a mechanical unfolding of genes to make sure the baby has a body with two arms, two legs, two eyes, etc. The next period of life is called the foetal stage, when the embryo has the human configuration. This phase, I like to call, the Head Start programme of Nature. Nature reads the environment and then adjusts the final tuning of the genetics of the child based on what's immediately going on in the world.'

Lipton also discusses the research of Thomas R. Verny who wrote the book *Nurturing Your Child from Conception*. Verny states, 'In fact, the great weight of the scientific evidence that has emerged over the last decade demands that we re-evaluate the mental and emotional abilities of unborn children. Awake or asleep, the studies show that unborn children are constantly tuned in to their mother's every action, thought and feeling. From the moment of conception, the experience in the womb shapes the brain and lays the groundwork for personality, emotional temperament, and the power of higher thought.'

Dr Lipton discusses new discoveries about the biochemical effects of the brain's functioning, which show that all the cells in one's body are affected by your thoughts. Our thoughts generate an emotion, a feeling that releases chemicals that affect all the cells in our body. These chemicals cross through the placenta to the baby. Scientists like Dr Bruce Lipton are today backing up what spiritual gurus of the past like Swami Vivekananda and modern day gurus like Deepak Chopra have been espousing.

What does Dr Lipton mean by this?

The baby's perception of the world is based on the environment the father and mother create, even when the baby is in the womb. I am sure you must have heard elderly women in your family saying that a pregnant woman should be happy, for a happy child to be born. The positivity that the mother radiates will ensure that the child imbibes the same. The mother passes on not just nutrition to the foetus, but also information about the environment, which then helps the baby modify his genetic programme so that he can ensure survival.

How does this affect me as a parent?

For the mother

It is essential for a woman who has just conceived a child to be content and feel secure about the conception and not be stressed. Nowadays, most women work right up to the ninth month of their pregnancy, which is fine as long as the work is engaging and stress free. The environment that the mother is in provides vital information to the baby about what to anticipate. If the mother is stressed out, the baby prepares for a stress-ridden life. A 6-month-old foetus is as intelligent and aware as a 1-year-old child! Even while agreeing that the fears in your mind regarding pregnancy and delivery are normal, these negative emotions develop an environment of fear for the child. Stay positive and enjoy the journey. The pregnancy journey is priceless.

For the father

If you think that your role starts only after the child is born, think again. The happy and relaxed environment that the mother needs for the baby is created by you. The father plays a very important role during the pre-natal period. Research shows that women who are not confident about their partner's support, financially or emotionally, tend to look at their pregnancy as unwanted. This negative approach towards the baby has far reaching effects.

Many first time fathers have problems developing a bond with someone that they haven't seen yet. If you accompany your partner to every pre-natal check up, you will find yourself bonding with the child. Soon you will be as excited about the birth as the mother. This is the time for you to prepare for how you are going to welcome your child. Remember, every

Enjoy Your Pregnancy

Generate positivity through your pregnancy by:

- meditating for a few minutes daily to maintain a calm state of mind;
- reflecting on how you are going through such wonderful changes;
- doing things that engage you;
- being in the present. Do not brood over the past or worry about the future; and
- watching your emotions and learning to handle them.

interaction you have with your partner adds to the subconscious download of the child.

The physical connect to emotional well being

It is often said you are what you eat. This is true for the mother-to-be and the child. The food that the mother eats has a direct impact on her emotions and, in turn, has an impact on her baby in the womb. That is why our grandmothers insist on satisfying the food cravings of pregnant women.

A lot is written on why food cravings occur during pregnancy and I intuitively believe that some of our cravings come from the wishes of our unborn child. I used to feel nauseous during my pregnancy whenever I ate any non-vegetarian food. My son at the age of 3 made the conscious decision to turn vegetarian. I believe that he was conceived with a vegetarian blueprint!

'I remember my mother and grandma would strictly monitor the food I ate when I was pregnant. I was kept off all fried food. They adamantly refused to use any refined products. My grandma had a very good explanation for all this. She used to say, "the fresher you eat, the fresher you feel, the happier you are, the happier your baby is!"' says Rashmi, 32, a filmmaker.

Ever feel like eating comfort food when something goes wrong? Food affects our mood. Knowing this can help a pregnant woman eat foods that keep her in a well balanced emotional state. 'Dietary changes can bring about changes in our brain structure (chemically and physiologically), which can lead to altered behaviour.

For example, the connection between carbohydrates and moods is all about tryptophan, a nonessential amino acid. As more tryptophan enters the brain, more serotonin is synthesized in the brain, and mood tends to improve. Serotonin, known as a mood regulator, is made naturally in the brain from tryptophan with some help from the B vitamins.[1] According to researchers from Arizona State University, a very low carbohydrate (ketogenic) diet was found to enhance fatigue. 'Foods thought to increase serotonin levels in the brain include fish and Vitamin D. Researchers from the University of Toronto noticed that people who were suffering from depression, particularly those with seasonal affective disorder, tended to improve as their Vitamin D levels in the body increased over the normal course of a year.'[2]

But it's important to make smart carbohydrate choices like whole grains, fruits, vegetables, and legumes, which also contribute important nutrients and fibre.

Ayurveda divides food into the categories satvik, rajasaic, and tamasik. Satvik food (like fruit, dairy products, legumes) is that which grows above the ground, is freshly prepared, energizes the body, and adds vitality. These foods induce a sense of fulfilment and contentment. Rajasaic are foods that are spicy and salty (like garlic, ginger, onion, tea and coffee) and induce emotions like hate and anger. Tamasik is food that is prepared with a lot of ghee, butter, and oil. Such foods can make one feel heavy and sleepy. Consumption of freshly prepared food that is light to digest helps you gain the required weight and ensures you have a happy pregnancy.

A newborn baby: The first few months

'I was sobbing. Did I create this beautiful baby from my own flesh and blood?'

'I had been totally busy with my work right up to the previous day. So the day I saw my baby, it actually struck me: Gosh! I am a mother now!'

'To be very honest, I was worried about how I was going to manage everything once I reached home. I had almost no support. I didn't know how to react!'

Every mother goes through different emotions after giving birth. All these varied reactions are normal.

I got married in December, 1989. Three months later, to my surprise and my husband's dismay, I discovered I was pregnant. Nine confused months later I went through 17 hours of labour to produce, what according to his father's words, looked like a rat! I knew I was supposed to feel this tremendous love and instant bond just like all the mothers in movies do as they scream in agony one moment and then gaze into their baby's eyes with unbridled adoration the next. I wanted to feel the same. In a sense I felt compelled to feel the same and found the reality of my actual emotional state spiralling me into guilt and despair. All I could feel was intense pain, exhaustion, and the need for sleep.

This may happen to you too. You will suddenly find that your entire life has gone through a massive change. A little 3-pound creature now rules your life. Every action is dictated by her. You wake when she wakes. You try to sleep when she does.

And for this very reason in India it was common to find that the new mother did not work for the first 40 days after delivery. This period helps a woman to recuperate from the physical and emotional upheaval that she is going through. But the pressures of the modern workplace have changed all these equations and mothers tend to get back to their jobs as soon as possible. In many families, this is an eventuality. There is no choice but to get back into the routine. In such a scenario, how can one balance both the pressure of caring for a new baby and their work life?

The answer is to prioritize. Your child is a baby only once in her lifetime. This is the stage when the child can get maximum inputs from you.

Raji, 33, says, 'I am a journalist and I shifted to freelancing once Kirtana was born. I knew I would not be able to dedicate the kind of time a full time job requires. So I decided to work from home. This gave me the space and time to be with her through her growing years. Kirtana now understands that the two hours I shut myself in my room, I am working and am not to be disturbed. I feel this has helped her in two ways. One, she knows that there is time when I need to be on my own.

Two, she *knows* that I am around and hence doesn't have any separation anxiety.'

With most offices working online and being connected 24×7, working from home is an option that the mothers of today can choose. Bond with your baby as frequently as you can. If you are working away from home, ensure that once you are back, you spend as much real time with your child as possible. Real time is interactive in nature. It can include a trip to the supermarket where you are observing things together on the way and where the child has a real task to accomplish at the supermarket. I used to print out or remove labels from food cans and bottles such as soup and corn tins and from the cardboard packaging such as food cereals and Kraft cheese as a visual shopping list. We would carry these on our trips to the food store and that was my son's shopping list. He would identify items like baked beans, milk, and cheese and drop them into the trolley. Every moment that you bond will enrich her subconscious bank. A few things to keep in mind:

1. **Breast feed your baby for as long as possible**: Research conducted in Japan shows that even the smell of the mother's milk is enough to calm irritated and angry babies. This is the most crucial time for your child, and a time to interact intimately with your baby. The bond that develops now will last a life time.

2. **Carry your baby around**: Having lived in the womb for nine months, babies crave for the same warmth. It is very reassuring for them to hear the familiar heartbeat. A calm and composed baby becomes a confident adult. The markets are full of swings, cribs, and baby bags. Keep them handy but hold on to your baby as long as you can. Research shows that babies who are carried around by their parents grow

up to be less clingy, happier, more intelligent, independent, loving, and social than babies who spend their time in infant seats, swings, and cribs.

3. **Let your baby sleep with you**: In India, as a culture, we follow the practice of co-sleeping. This is gradually decreasing nowadays. In the West, co-sleeping is considered dangerous because of the instances of infant deaths. However, the number of infant deaths is high more because of the carelessness of the adult and not because the practice itself is dangerous. Most mothers find it easy to co-sleep with the baby as feeding the baby becomes easier. Also, this allows the mother to be more aware of what is happening with the baby. Working mothers too find co-sleeping beneficial as it gives them quality time with their child.

4. **Listen to the language of your baby**: Each baby has a unique way of communicating. Observe how your baby cries, laughs, gurgles. They will give you an indication of if she is hungry, wet, angry, tired, sleepy, or happy.

5. **A healthy baby needs a healthy mother**: Ensure you keep yourself healthy and happy. A tired, worried, and over-worked mother cannot contribute positively to the development of a happy baby.

I am a working mom

Guilt is the most common feeling that most working mothers feel. As I understand, guilt comes from not just having to leave the child at home but also to leave work to nurse a sick child.

I have experienced guilt when I left baby Drish to start my own school. But that I feel is the part of the life of every mother. A woman who has had a stay-at-home mom usually goes through the feeling of guilt at a higher level than the one who has grown up under someone who went out to work.

What a working mother needs to ensure is that the child experiences varied interactions that allow language and emotional development to take place. These experiences could be with grandparents or the caregivers. It's always useful to let the grandparents take charge of the children when the mother is out of the home. There are many women who feel that grandparents can pamper the children rotten. Rules of discipline can be discussed among the adults of the family to ensure that all speak the same voice. The other option would be to hire well trained caregivers. This may be tough at times, but you need to ensure that the person whom you entrust your child with is exactly that—trustworthy. Hiring someone who has done an Early Childhood course for example may be hired for a few hours a day so that she engages the child in a variety of child appropriate activities. Ensure that you create an atmosphere of interaction once you are back from work. Plan picnics with other young mothers so that your children can not only interact with kids their age, but also with other adults.

I was talking to a group of working mothers in Bhopal. Each one of them felt intensely guilty and sensed disapproval from their mothers and mothers-in-law. I asked them if they had thought of productive and helpful options such as an extended day care service? This group of mothers convinced their employers to allow them to work any five days of their choice. So now each mother runs a day care once a week for five children, with home cooked meals and involve the kids in age appropriate games and activities. The toddlers are not only having fun, but also gaining from the experience, and, of course, the mothers love the fact that they can spend time with the children. When they are at work they are at peace that their children are with someone they trust.

Studies conducted by the American Psychological Association (1999) and the University of Texas show that there are no developmental problems in children whose mothers worked outside the home. Dr Aletha Huston, director of the research, states, 'The mother is an important source of care, but then she doesn't have to be there twenty-four hours a day to build a strong relationship with her child. Children are not affected by the mother's absence. In fact what impacts the child is her personality and her beliefs, her values, and the time she spends with them. Staying at home is not the issue. Staying with the kid is.'

When talking about the working mother's impact on children, we must realize how differently working mothers and stay-at-home mothers view discipline. Mothers who are at home usually tend to use either a more demanding or lenient approach to parenting than those who are working. Working mothers are more likely to use an approach that relies on reason, trust, and convincing power than the use of authoritative parental power. As compared to their counterparts, working mothers are found to differentiate less between sons and daughters in their disciplining styles and goal setting skills. Working mothers also value the independence of their daughters more than stay-at-home moms.

Families with working mothers have different dynamics between the father's and the families—fathers are more involved with the daily running of the household. They are more connected to their children as they realize the need to partner their responsibilities. They do not blindfoldedly leave everything to their wives. Daughters with such fathers tend to have a greater sense of personal achievement.

The debate whether mothers should set out of home or sit at home will continue and we may or may not agree with the research. I think that working mothers feel a sense of empowerment, and, in turn, their confidence rubs off on the children in great measure. I believe that my son's work ethic comes from me even though he must have felt neglected sometimes just like I had my pangs of guilt. Would he have felt short changed at times as a child? I am sure he did, but I am also sure that today he will say that having a working mother has more positives than negatives. Sometimes, as a woman, it is easier if you *have* to work for economic reasons rather than when you *choose* to work. Drish has worked out his mantra or calling to 'Be the voice of the common man in India' and whether he does this through acting or any other means, I have no doubt that he will live up to his purpose. True self fulfilment only happens when you have a purpose and work towards making it a reality.

There is a great deal of data pertaining to the influence of a self employed parent or an aspiring entrepreneur. A 30-year-old longitudinal study at the Institute of Personality Assessment and Research, University of California, of a database of architects found that those who had acquired high levels of self-reliance at an early age were typically raised in an environment with one or more parents who were self employed. Young people steeped in such environments grow up to be more self-reliant, confident, resilient, and competent to make their own way in life. Conversely, when the income earning parent or parents work as employees, the offspring is more likely to seek employment rather than pursue entrepreneurial ventures.

Television as the babysitter

Unknown to most of us, children left in the care of maids are often left to passively be cared for and stimulated by the television set. I have often cringed at the sight of food being shoved inside a toddler's mouth as he watches TV. Not only do these children have their brain switches of hunger and sustenance numbed by eating and watching TV at the same time, these toddlers will most likely develop incorrect eating habits and adult obesity. In trying to reverse this cycle, I once counselled a woman whose child refused to eat. Each time this would happen she would switch on the TV because it acted as a tool for distraction and her child ate. My advice was simple. 'Never has a healthy child been known to die of hunger in the presence of food. You simply need to allow the triggers to kick back in.'

The advice is simple. Stop running after your child with a food plate and stop feeding your child while he is distracted by toys or the television. Make meal times a family affair. Your child may skip a few meals if used to a distracted eating style but as long as you do not give in to in between meal snacking to compensate he will quickly fall into conscious mindful eating. What you will have accomplished is a lifetime of healthy eating habits, a tendency to know hunger and full signals, and an avoidance of your child ever turning into a couch potato.

The first two years (1 to 2)

Energizing the synapses

The brain is the only organ that is not completely developed at birth. All the other organs continue to grow after the child is born. But the brain continues to *develop* after birth.

The development of the child's brain has a lot to do with the experiences she undergoes. The child has millions of brain cells when born. Each experience creates a synapse in her brain. A synapse is a connection between the various cells of the brain. Like a bulb it will work only if a source of energy is present. When there is no electricity, a bulb won't glow. Once the power supply is ensured, the bulb continues to glow till the power is taken away from the bulb. Similarly, the synapse needs a continuous supply of input to remain active.

This connection happens with *every* single activity. The more experiences we offer a baby, the more synaptic connections she is able to make. These connections between the cells help develop the brain, and so they need to be nurtured and motivated. Synapses that are not fed with thought and action will die. That is why we learn certain things and forget others. So use every opportunity you get to keep synapses active.

What does this mean for me as a parent?

Very frequently I have had parents ask me, 'Will my baby understand if I read stories to her now? She is just eight months.'

Yes, of course, she will! You underestimate the power of the human brain. Remember Prahlad in Chapter 4. He is dyslexic but a voracious reader nevertheless. His mother read stories to him every night from the time he was a baby. Today he has read so much that he says, 'I know everything about everything I read.'

How will I know which synapse is active and which is not?

Surely that's not possible and that is why we need to ensure that we provide a varied environment for our children.

Show the baby a rattle. Rub her back. Tickle her. Show them paintings, cartoons, pictures, take them out, read to them, sing to them, play the drums, the guitar, the piano. Each of these trigger different synapses. All these simple activities add to the synaptic connections the baby is making. Every activity you do may lay the foundation for some talent, which will surface later in life.

With every synaptic connection it is not just the intelligence of the brain that develops, important emotional growth such as trust in the parent begins during the first year too. Let your baby bathe in your love. The more interaction you offer her as a parent, the more confident she grows as an adult.

What sort of an environment do I provide for my baby?

You don't need to redo your entire apartment to suit the baby. A few simple steps and a little care go a long way.

1. **Food**: Healthy food is vital. Stay away from readily available formula food as far as possible. Just as you took care of yourself during the pregnancy, ensure the baby has healthy food. The food needs to be climate specific. Food that suits the climate of the place is easily digested. Avoid trying things because your sister in the UK is doing the same. The climatic requirements of each place are different.

2. **Sleep**: The brain organizes and reorganizes stuff when the baby sleeps. Sleep and sleep cycles are very essential to develop the sensory skills of a child. Research has shown that the following sensory systems need adequate sleep beginning at as early as the foetal stage.

Somatesthetic	Touch
Kinesthetic	Motion
Proprioception	Position
Chemosensory	Smell and taste
Auditory	Hearing
Vision	Sight
Limbic	Emotion
Social learning	Social Skills
Hippocampus	Memory

A word of caution: Most adults with sleep difficulties have usually been trained into being able to sleep only if the ideal conditions for sleep are available. I always advise that children get used to sleeping on a variety of soft and hard surfaces, with a mixture of light and sound in the environment. I know adults who cannot sleep unless they have the correct mattress or pillow density and touch and others who cannot do so in the presence of even a sliver of light or sound as they have been trained to sleep 'just so'.

We, in our anxiety for the child, may be doing them a disservice by providing 'ideal' conditions.

3. **Water**: A thirsty brain doesn't think. Eighty percent of the child's brain is made of water. Water is highly essential for the child's brain. Every thought that comes in the brain of the child is a chemical or electrical reaction! These reactions need water. If children don't have enough water, their brains become sluggish.

4. **Safety**: Humans instinctively try to keep themselves safe. If the baby feels that its priority is to be safe, then its brain will

concentrate only on that, leaving little time for learning. So let your baby feel that she doesn't have to worry about fending for herself.

5. **Space**: Kids need space. Give them as much of it as you can. If your house is small, ensure that they get to play outside. Take them to gardens, beaches, parks, etc.

6. **Plants**: Include plants in their space. Plants give oxygen, which is fuel for the brain.

Capture the windows of opportunity

'My mother-in-law would keep talking to my baby Rujuta all day long. The baby would coo and my mother-in-law would answer in full sentences. I asked her if she felt that Rutuja was following what she said. She replied that she had been taught by her mom that the only way children learnt how to talk was when someone kept talking to them,' says Geeta.

Geeta's mother-in-law didn't know the science behind it but she was bang on. At times we feel that since kids only coo and babble, they don't understand what we tell them so we end up talking gibborish. This makes kids believe that baby talk is right. *Kids who are used to baby talk are then prone to use it even later as it takes them longer to unlearn it.* It is better to expose kids to the regular, normal way of talking right from the beginning.

The synapses relating to language skills develop the maximum between the ages of 1 to 3 years, which is the time during which a child learns to speak. However, new languages can be learnt at any time in a person's life; the synapses of language learning can always be restored. The brain uses the first language learnt as a foundation for the second or third

Avoid Overstimulation

There was a recent Baby Einstein craze in the US which had many mothers parking their toddlers in front of a video believing the claims that the video would make the baby smarter. In the latest study on the effects of popular videos such as 'Baby Einstein' and 'Brainy Baby', researchers found that these products may be doing more harm than good. And they may actually delay language development in toddlers.

Led by Frederick Zimmerman and Dr Dimitri Christakis, both at the University of Washington, the research team found that with every hour per day spent watching baby DVDs and videos, infants learned six to eight fewer words than babies who never watched the videos. These products had the strongest detrimental effect on babies 8 to 16 months old, the age at which language skills start to form.

'Babies require face-to-face interaction to learn,' says Dr Vic Strasburger, professor of paediatrics at the University of New Mexico School of Medicine and a spokesperson for the American Academy of Paediatrics. 'They don't get that interaction from watching TV or videos. In fact, the watching probably interferes with the crucial wiring being laid down in their brains during early development.'

'As far as Christakis and his colleagues can determine, the only thing that baby videos are doing is producing a generation of overstimulated kids. His group has found that the more television children watch, the shorter their attention spans are later in life. "Their minds come to expect a high level of stimulation, and view that as normal," says Christakis, "and by comparison, reality is boring."'[3]

In our anxiety to be perfect, we tend to overstimulate. Do not keep the baby awake for too long. She needs her sleep. Too many activities, too many new smells, food items, too many people; all cause overstimulation. This stresses out the child.

language and places the new language in comparison to the older ones.

The brain does not feed all the skills at the same time. Dr John Medina, a developmental molecular biologist, has been researching how the mind reacts to and organizes information for years. In his book *The Brain Rules* he states that the brain is incapable of multi-tasking. Hence, different skills develop at different times. The age when these skills develop in a child are called 'the windows of opportunity'.

The window for motor skills and math also open around the same time as language and remain open through life. Simple activities which help to identify few and many, little and more, help develop an interest in math and logic.

Let your child be your guide

'When Aditi was around 3 years old, I took her to a Bharatnatyam class. The guruji told me very clearly that he would admit her only once she turned 5. I still remember him saying that it's only at this age that children are able to do complex dance steps. Their mind and body should be equally ready. Today Aditi is 15 and I can proudly say a very graceful dancer,' says Mayura, 40, an event manager.

Many parents ask me the 'right' age for their children to start learning an activity. I tell them that the trick is to 'let your child guide you'. People who succeed at something need resilience and motivation; the ability to maintain a bottomless effort supply. A youngster who is forced to attend Bharatnatyam classes for an hour every day is unlikely to become an accomplished dancer. But a child who loves dancing, is interested in dancing, and understands the potential of success will prioritize and complete her practice sessions and is more likely to become a proficient and successful dancer. The advice I give parents is to keep opening windows of opportunities for their children—sport, musical instruments, theatre, dance, everything—and allowing them to decide what they like and want to pursue.

When my son, Drish, was 4 years old, he and I were holidaying in Maldives where we attended a Benetton fashion show. The event organizers asked if Drish would walk the ramp with the other models and he readily agreed. At the show, I saw him confidently walk the ramp, his excitement and attitude coming through. At that moment I realized that a star had been born. Today, he has gone on to do advertisements, a television show, and recently completed a course in acting.

Malcolm Gladwell in *The Outliers: The Story of Success* mentions the '10,000-Hour Rule', claiming that the key to success in any field is in practising a specific task for a total of 10,000 hours. To put aside that much time one needs a large unending reservoir of resilience, motivation, and commitment, which can only happen if the person enjoys the activity in the first place.

But the most important window of opportunity that opens at this time is that of the development of emotional bonding. The child bonds with the parents, the grandparents, and friends at this time. Utilize this to the maximum. *The areas of trust build from birth to 2 years. Those who are able to build trust in these two years turn to be very caring adults themselves later on.*

How will my child grow to trust me?

- **Physical space**: Keep the environment of the child clean. If the baby has wet or soiled himself, clean up immediately. Feed the child every two hours, set alarms if required.
- **Emotional space**: Kids cry not only when they are hungry

or dirty, they have emotional needs too. So pay attention to your child's tears, she may just want to be held tight or need a little comforting.

- **The mind space**: Babies and toddlers will lead you; give you clues as to what they want. Follow them. They know when they are hungry or not, angry or not, tired or not. Learn to pick up the cues. When you do that, the baby learns to trust you.

Children Learn Best When:

- learning is through hands-on activities, songs, games, and interaction with others;
- through themes or things that are of relevance and interest to them; and
- instruction is customized to each child's unique needs, since children have preferred ways of learning. Some children may learn best by seeing; some are good listeners, while others are kinesthetic learners. (This instruction customization is applicable not only when teaching a toddler. Yelling 'be quiet' may work for an auditory child but a visual child may need to watch you instruct him through your actions that you want him to calm down and a kinesthetic child may actually need you to go across the room and touch him till he calms down.

Whenever the above points are kept in mind, children learn quickly, thoroughly, and almost on their own. They acquire a life-long thirst for learning. True learning only takes place when the brain is confronted with a problem to solve. Preparing learners to be challenged by problems to solve heightens the learning experience. A teacher or parent should play the role of one who orchestrates the learning experience rather than directing it.

The terrible 2s

'NO!'

That is the one word which summarizes this period of a child's life.

The behaviour of a child is based on his emotions rather than logic. At the age of 2, children develop a sense of the self and realize that they have a separate identity vis à vis their parents. They realize they have the capacity to do certain things independently and that what they want might be different from what you want them to do. This conflict creates anger and frustration and finally tantrums. And everyone has seen a 2-year-old throw a fit!

Children at this age are not being defiant or rebellious. They are just trying to express their independence. Their language skills haven't yet developed and, hence they use the physical responses and may bite, hit or resort to temper tantrums. My son had a habit of turning on and turning off the television set (most natural as he was exploring the cause effect theory!) I tried telling him not to which of course only made him do it more! One day I simply unplugged the television. He tried it that day and the next and then simply shrugged his shoulders, gave me a questioning glance before murmuring 'Mumma, not working' and went on to find his next adventure.[4]

The terrible 2s are a major milestone in the life of your child. They are tumultuous and simmering. At the same time, they are exhilarating and exuberant. Enjoy this time with your child.

Tips to Tackle the Terrible 2s

- **Stick to a routine**: Maintain a routine for naps, meals, play time, bedtime, bath, etc. Routine brings stability in the child's mind. He then begins to anticipate the next activity and learns to get ready for it. You will notice that when it's bath time, he may get his towel and soap ready for you.

- **Offer choices**: Don't ask open ended, questions like, 'What juice do you want to drink?' Instead ask 'do you want orange or lemon juice?' Being able to choose gives your 2-year-old a sense of independence. He is given the freedom to choose. This makes him feel in charge and powerful.

- Don't give in to tantrums.

- Don't just say 'no'. Say what they could do instead of that.

- Distract them. It's easy to get kids to do different things.

- Make most things seem like a game. They could aim to throw waste paper into the trash can.

- Count on stars and smileys to reward them. They love it when they are rewarded.

- A safe environment is highly essential. Ensure that any fragile or delicate things are out of their reach. The home need not turn into a war field.

The Beginning of Learning

A mistake is a crash-course in learning.
Billy Anderson

The fun theory

I take a huge interest in what children are interested in because I believe that if you can find what catches a child's fancy or what engages a child the most—an inroad to 'fun'—then you can teach them any concept or skill through that interest. And this works for adults too. I instantly knew that I could teach English, science, history or math to Pratham by using cars because, well, he liked cars.

High interest translates into a higher focus or concentration level. We all know that when we focus the rays of the sun through a magnifying glass on a piece of paper, the paper catches fire. Similarly energy is maximized on what we focus.

There is an interesting experiment conducted to try and get people to use a staircase instead of the escalator that I show parents and teachers. This can be accessed at www.thefuntheory. com/piano-staircase. A group of people tried to see if people could be motivated to do a difficult thing if it is made fun. So they chose a place where there was a flight of steps and an escalator. They painted the steps like the keys of a piano and wired it so that it would produce music when stepped on. Soon people began using the stairs instead of the escalator because that proved to be more fun. This proved that a difficult task, if made fun, is preferred over an easier one.

The fun theory is the basis for all the learning methodology we use in our schools and is something that can be used for parenting as well. Can't get kids to cooperate at home? You want them to keep their room clean? Set the table? You can find a way to turn any chore into a game with a stop watch, score card, or any other gaming strategy.

Positive and negative energy

I had recently gone to visit an aunt who stays in a retirement home. The place was nice and she said she was happy, but there was one small thing that irritated her. The plastic bucket chairs provided by the institute had wedges in them and she found it uncomfortable sitting on them. I told her to focus on what she was doing while she was sitting on the chair instead of thinking about the chair itself, and that in no time she would forget where she was sitting. A week later she called me to tell me that the trick had worked. When she concentrated on reading what she was reading or watching TV programmes she forgot that she was even sitting on a chair!

Energy naturally flows to the point we focus.

Divya, one of my colleagues, says, 'I realized the power of negative energy when my son, Pavan, began to study abroad. The first time he was leaving, I had warned him to keep his passport carefully. I told him, "Get photocopies made and be careful or else you will lose your passport." And that's exactly what happened! He lost his passport and reached an hour late. He missed the flight and I was poorer by another Rs 40,000 getting him on the next flight.'

Another colleague of mine, Deepa constantly finds insects in her food. I tell her she finds them because she is subconsciously looking for them.

'I am dyslexic,' advertising guru, Prahlad Kakkar said to me, 'and as a kid, we never knew what being dyslexic was or meant. Through school I was considered to be an average student and my grandfather used to berate me for being the black sheep in the family. But my mom read a lot to me and I would disappear into my imaginary world. I was a huge day dreamer. In my dreams, I came up with all kinds of solutions for all kind of problems. Where my reading ended my fantasies began. Thus, there was so much focus on fantasy in my mind that it was not surprising that I found my niche in the field of advertising and creativity. Aren't we selling fantasies to our customers?'

The more negative we are about something, the higher the chances of it turning out negative. So if the focus is positive, the energy flow will also be positive.

My entire philosophy of education and parenting has developed from my observations and personal experiences. I watched an older brother excel academically but struggle socially and emotionally. On the other hand, I watched my younger brother Kamal scoring bottom of the barrel grades and failing his HSC twice. When we were growing up in Australia, a certain brand of chocolate became quite a fad because you got free football cards with it. Kamal, who was passionate about football, desperately wanted to get his hands on all of them. But mom would give him only one. He began to trade the cards and soon collected almost a hundred. He would spend hours on the pot imagining a football game with his own commentary. His commentaries were so loud and entertaining that we would patiently wait for him to wind up the entire match!

Today, my older brother still has a 'highly valued at school' brilliant left brain but will always play second fiddle to the leadership that my younger brother enjoys due to the negotiation capabilities and gift of the gab he developed while role playing football commentaries. Does this mean I advocate not applying oneself academically? The answer is a resounding NO! What I would have liked is a schooling and parenting system that could have helped my older brother develop socially and one that used my younger brother's interest in football to teach him math, English, history, and even physics in a fun and interesting way.

Left brainers vs right brainers

My brothers, one a left brainer and the other a right brainer, motivated me to study more about this concept and I will share with you what I have learnt about how the two parts of the brain work independently and inter-dependently. Knowing this will help us understand how our kids are wired and what we need to do for them to be successful in the future.

Left brainers are analytical, systematic, logical, and sequential. They are good at math and science. They love to stay indoors and handle systems. Left brainers are generally better at written communication but not too good at marketing themselves or talking about themselves. Since they are process oriented, they are not very adept at marking out their own skills and talents. They also find it difficult to quantify their contributions. They usually prefer their own company.

Right brainers are creative, intuitive, and emotional. They are good speakers and can organize events. They enjoy writing and art. Right brainers love to talk to people and work in groups. A creative person looks for a lot of self acceptance from what he does. From this self acceptance arises the concept of self-esteem. As they are creative people they have high self-esteem issues when it comes to asking for help from others. It's difficult for them to maintain inventories of their achievements.

Bestselling author and journalist Daniel Pink in his book *Why Right Brainers Will Rule the World* observes that the 21st century is witnessing a shift in what is required of people at the fastest rate. Calculating and tabulating numbers with speed and accuracy was once a prized skill. However, every kid today knows that a calculator or an excel worksheet can do the same thing faster and definitely more accurately.

The Internet has made the globe flat. People and places are no longer divided by time or defined by space. Better lifestyles, growing affluence, and changing socio-cultural and economic patterns are causing unprecedented challenges in human evolution and development. So parenting and teaching styles and techniques need to match the demands of the ever evolving society. Pink anoints this current trend as the Conceptual Age and its movers and shakers as the creative thinkers who can empathize with others standpoints and solve problems on the spot. He justifies this change in these words:

'...In short, we've progressed from a society of farmers to a society of factory workers to a society of knowledge workers. And now we're progressing yet again—to a society of creators and empathisers, of pattern recognizers and meaning makers.'[1]

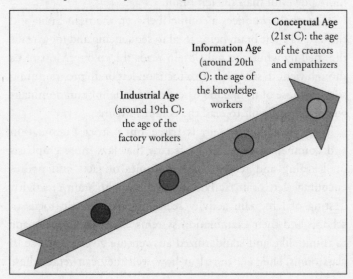

Conceptual Age (21st C): the age of the creators and empathizers

Information Age (around 20th C): the age of the knowledge workers

Industrial Age (around 19th C): the age of the factory workers

How do I know if I am a right brainer?

You can do a small but interesting test to check if you are a right brainer or a left brainer. Go to http://www.perthnow.com.au/fun-games/left-brain-vs-right-brain/story-e6frg46u-1111114517613. The page shows a lady spinning on her foot. Look at the image carefully. If you see her spinning clockwise then you are a right brainer. If you see her spinning anti-clockwise then you are a left brainer. You will also notice that after sometime she begins to spin in the opposite direction of what you have been seeing. This is because the other side of your brain has been activated by that time. Soon you will be able to decide which side she can spin. If you think clockwise, she will spin clockwise.

Or try the 'Left or right brained?' experiment later in the book. Look at the chart and try reading the colour of the word. If you are easily able to read the colours, your right brain is more powerful than the left brain.

The chart produces a conflict between the right brain and the left. The left brain being used to sequencing and logic reads the spelling while the right brain reads the colour. Most of us though went to schools with a focus on left brain programming so even those of us like me who are more right brain dominant will find it difficult to read the colour initially.

Our education system is based on a strict examination and commensurate grading systems that lays more emphasis on learning and remembering volumes of facts and figures encourage left brain activity and stunt right brain creativity. Testing of left brain activity seems to be the main focus of schools and their examination systems. All students are made to think alike and standardized answers are given en masse in classrooms. They are tested in how well they can retain these answers. It's not a surprise that Einstein once remarked: 'The only thing that interferes with my learning is my education.'

This is why left brain dominated children do well in school, as they are more likely to respond to formal learning. They exhibit greater responsibility, are quite content studying by themselves, and have greater concentration. The right brain child may not be an academically inclined in the classroom. They like to work in groups, usually restless, they prefer to be free rather than be tied up in a formal classroom.

If right brain skills are not exercised at all, there is a possibility that children may not develop sufficiently. A well built curriculum, which subscribes to the development of both the sides of the brain, is thus the requirement of the day. Activities that encourage various creative skills hone the right brain thinking process to provide emotional and visual vignettes and freely associated images. Kids then associate these images with their thoughts and find patterns to understand problems and gaps. Too much logical dominance in any creative process helps the left brain assert itself and dispense most creative ideas as irrational and unpractical.

However, I like to believe that it is important to develop practical means to train both the hemispheres sufficiently so that their average intelligence and creativity can be raised to a much higher level. If today, we as parents, educators, and mentors collectively take up this task, our children will grow up to be musicians, scholars, scientists, and researchers who will enrich our cultural heritage.

One's dominant brain type has a very significant effect on one's study skills, homework habits, and grades too. That is why while some students struggle with certain type of test questions, others sail through with élan. **For example, students who are left brain dominant will answer short objective**

questions a lot better than their right brain dominant counterparts who will answer narrative questions with more dexterity. By understanding our children's dominant brain type, we can guide them to adjust their study methods and chalk out their study schedule and course work to suit their own personality type.

Many people who eventually find right brain success go through failure. French sculptor Auguste Rodin was rejected from art school three times. Walt Disney was fired from a newspaper he worked for 'because he lacked imagination and had no original ideas'! Too often right brain people are viewed and judged from a left brain perspective.

If my right brain dominant student is having trouble understanding a math concept, I will explain the concept to him through a story or manipulate some art work or materials to help him understand. In this way I believe we can help any child use his/her strengths to gain insights into a difficult problem that he cannot crack on his own. We must remember that a child can whole heartedly engage in learning only if we as parents and teachers assist each other to make his workload meaningful and fun. In the forthcoming chapters I will discuss more about this from the standpoint of Howard Gardner's Theory of Multiple Intelligence and other approaches.

Most of us are trained to be left brain dominant by our educational system. Our policy is 'one size fits all'. We don't 'manage' problems like right-brainers, we 'solve' them, even if that entails trampling over others. We don't know what 'tact' is. Rajesh, a 35-year-old banker, remembers the time when he as an eighth grader and went to his father with a math problem the night before the exam; he was first scolded for coming at the eleventh hour and then his father began to clear his concepts from scratch—telling him all about the 'why,' 'what,' 'when,' 'which' and 'how' of the matter (in the process confusing him even further).

A right brained parent would have tackled the situation in a different way. He would have taken into consideration the constraint of time at hand and explained only the 'how' of the matter to Rajesh and set him free to fend for himself, leaving him with two little encouraging phrases—'Trust me, you'll make it. Just believe in yourself.' When a child is already in an anxious state of mind little else can be done.

Tune in to the mind and the body

There is a very popular story about Yesudas, the famous Indian classical singer, who was once travelling on an airplane. He realized a change in the sound of the engines and immediately brought this to the notice of the crew. The pilot realized that one of the engines was having trouble and requested for an emergency landing. The journey continued an hour late with a more relived set of passengers.

Human beings are born with the ability to see, hear, taste, feel, and smell. Learning happens not because of just one of these senses but because all of them work together.

The brain receives hundreds and thousands of bits and pieces of information in a day. What does the brain do with all this? It sorts them and stores them into various folders, which then are pulled up at the required time.

Garima is a fashion designer. She will be able to tell you what fabric is in her hand just by touching it. This is because of the innumerable times she has touched various fabrics and her brain has stored these inputs for her to use.

You know when your dal needs more salt in it, even if you have never cooked it. How? Your brain has used the sense of taste and figured out how much salt you need in your dal.

So that's how sensory motor integration works. It is imperative to ensure appropriate sensory motor integration as it has far reaching consequences on children.

Keeping both left and right brain connected

Simple activities can ensure all round development of both the left and right brain.

The sense of sight: Children love to see bright colours. Keep their toys within their line of vision. This will motivate them to try to pick them up. When they are toddlers, point out to colourful objects so that they can follow your finger and look at the object. Hang pictures of family members so that they begin to identify them even if they do not see them on a daily basis. Take them out to the park or the garden. Give them as much visual input as possible.

The sense of sound: Sing to them. Talk to them. Play good music. Hang wind chimes so that the breeze brings with it soothing sounds into the house. Read aloud books. Children as young as 4 or 5 months love to be read to.

The sense of taste: This sense develops when the child is in the womb. It depends a lot on what the mother eats during her pregnancy. The first thing a child should taste, however, is mother's milk. Introduce new tastes one at a time. Avoid confusing the child by introducing too many tastes at the same time. Research shows that children can't taste salt till they are 4 months old.

The sense of smell: Children are very perceptive with this one. A newborn identifies the mother by her smell. That is why most children stop crying when they are handled by the mother. The child identifies with the smell of the mother, something he has carried with him from the womb. This smell is what gives him a level of comfort. As they begin to breastfeed they identify with the smell of milk too. The sense of smell, in later years, can be heightened by introducing kids to various smells, fragrant or otherwise. Get your child to register the smell of fresh flowers, the fragrance of the wet mud on the first day of the rains, the pungent smell of onions, the spices in curries, etc.

The sense of touch: This is a very important sensory input. Children feel comforted when they are touched by the ones who love them. Children can feel the emotion of the person carrying them. Give them toys of different kinds, fabrics of different textures to feel and play.

The right and left hemispheres of a child need to be trained to cross relate to each other. Each and every activity that you encourage with sensory inputs will add to the cross linking. Children who do not have adequate exposure to sensory motor integration usually have psychomotor disadvantages later on in life. Children may turn out to be over or under sensitive, hyperactive or underactive or in a state of constant or no motion.

The simple fun activities that I have enumerated earlier will help you keep the senses of your child open to stimulation.

How do I ensure that my child uses all the senses to the optimum?

There is a chance that as the child grows she may slowly reduce the use of one or more of the senses, limiting the potential of the brain. As a parent you can inculcate certain habits in your children that will last a lifetime.

1. **Teach them to see and not just look**: Bring out patterns, styles, minor perfections in things. This will teach them to observe and not just glance at things.

2. **Teach them to hear and not just listen**: Read aloud whenever they are exposed to something new. Even reading a passage from a newspaper will help. Play good music and encourage them to pay attention to the lyrics and enjoy the intricacies of music. Music is known to develop a very strong bank of emotions.

3. **Teach them to write down stuff**: Get your children to maintain a diary. Let them write thank you notes or letters to loved ones. Encourage them to write stories, poems, and notes in class. The more they write, the better things get etched in the memory and the better the sensory integration as this involves vision, hand movement, and thought.

4. **Draw, sketch, map things out**: The more they learn schematic representation, the more aware they become of clues that will tell them what to look out for when they are observing things.

5. **Creative visualization**: Imagination is a strong tool. The more developed the power of imagination in a child, the better equipped he is to deal with the abstract. Once he develops the skill of visualizing abstract concepts, such as

when your child reads a storybook he visualizes the setting of the story, he will find it easier to deal with reality. In the movie *Baby's Day Out*, the baby is able to relate to all the places he goes to because he has seen the pictures of these places. When the picture in the mind matches the picture in reality, identification become easier.

6. **Children enjoy research:** Take them through books; show them images on the Internet. Give them a project and let them search for information. The fun of hunting for information and the joy at finding it gives them a heightened level of achievement.

7. **Encourage mind games:** like crosswords, Sudoku, joining the dots, finding the differences, etc.

8. **Let them question:** Do not rebuke them. Only a questioning mind thrives.

Give your child every opportunity to imbibe the best through all the senses. If we analyze our religious practices, irrespective of what they are, we will notice that each one gives equal emphasis to all the senses. The fragrance of the incense sticks, the touch of water and earth, the flavours of different food items, the sounds of the bells, and the cries of worship… all cater to each one of the senses. Besides the religious element attached to these and you will see the science and rationale behind why these rituals exist.

First day in pre-school

For many parents, the first day at school may represent your child's first step toward independence. But for kids, this can be a very scary day. New faces, new surroundings, and the absence of the parent—a potent mixture to induce anxieties in him. How do you transition your child into a pre-school easily?

- Talk to him about school in advance. Prepare him for the fact that he has to go to school. Be positive in your descriptions of the school.
- Read out stories in which kids begin to go to school.
- Prepare him for the separation. Send him to spend some time with the grandparents or to a friend's place.
- Plan a visit to the school. Show him around the school, especially the play area. Get his teacher to meet him regularly for a few days prior to the first day.
- Get him into a routine. If school starts at eight in the morning begin to wake him up at seven so that he will be ready to leave. Get him to do some activity like drawing or colouring so that he gets into the routine of a school-like timetable.
- Most pre-schools have a settling time for the children. Find out what they plan to do. They may allow you to remain in school for some time. During this time encourage him to participate in the activities. Do not spend too much time with him when in class.
- On the other hand spend as much time as possible with your child before he leaves for school on the first day.
- Do not creep away from him. Though easier to do, the child will learn to mistrust you. Wish him a clear good bye. Say that you will be back by snack time. Till then the teacher will take care of him.
- If he cries loudly, and tries to cling on to you, be strong and let GO. Otherwise, he will fall into a pattern of crying just to make sure you stay with him. Instruct the school to call you in case of an emergency.

- Be punctual when you come to fetch him. He believes you will be back at snack time. Then be back by then. Don't let him down.
- In a week he will be raring to go and wanting to reach school faster than you could ever imagine!

The School Years and Learning in New Ways

I am always ready to learn although I do not always like being taught.

Winston Churchill

Your child is now reaching the most important part of his childhood—the school years. This age dominates a large part of the child's life. Memories of school will remain with him forever, entwined with memories of his childhood. Friends, teachers, classrooms, laboratories, projects, school camps, etc., should all form a wonderful reservoir of memories. But we must understand the difference between giving our children an education and the process of learning.

The power of conceptual thought

Did you know that Steve Jobs, the legendary chief executive of Apple Inc. and inventor of the Apple Mac, iPod, iPhone, and the oh-so-cool iPad never graduated from college? On June 12, 2005, he gave a commencement address at Stanford University titled 'You've got to find what you love'. He told students about the time he dropped out of college, but continued to attend the lectures that interested him without bothering about test results or a degree on paper. He went where curiosity and intuition led him, to calligraphy classes without hope of calligraphy ever having a practical application in his life. Many years later his knowledge of calligraphy helped him design the bestselling Apple Mac personal computer. 'If I had never dropped out, I would never have dropped in on this calligraphy class, and personal computers might not have the wonderful typography they do now,' he said.

Divya's (my colleague) experience with her son, Pavan, is very interesting. He attended an SSC school. In all terms of the word her son was a brat—both in school and at home. Divya was always worried about what he may do next. I encouraged her to see Pavan for the bright spark he really was, simply disengaged at school because there were no dots to connect, no meaning he could attach to what he was learning and was being a terror at home because he was forced to connect the dots through homework he saw no meaning in. The moment Pavan left his SSC school and began studying in New Zealand, we have a boy we no longer recognize. He is engaged at school, and has chosen to work after school on his own.

The prerequisites of the Conceptual Age include out-of-the-box thinking, and encouraging learners to follow their own intuition and instinct. It's the key to bringing back the magic of learning. Forget about learning and teaching materials, and pedagogies designed to improve test scores. Move away from the restrictive atmospheres of classrooms and head towards the open gardens instead. Fall in love with creativity, imagination, ingenuity, and the intuition of young minds.

An integrated and interdisciplinary system of teaching

'I was born intelligent. The education system ruined me.' Mark Twain's famous quote is true for many educational systems around the world. Kids enter schools as curious and inquisitive creatures and leave the portals as unthinking, uncreative, and undemanding people. This is what prompted me to start schools that would use brain research and innovative teaching methodologies to ensure that kids turn out to be thinking, creative, and demanding individuals.

Currently most of the learning and teaching materials and pedagogies employed in India are designed to improve test scores, whereas the objective should be the development of love of learning in young minds, which need to be opened up to the beauty and wonders of science, literature, mathematics, and languages. For students to become engaged with learning history, math or any other subject, they must be awakened to the meaning or purpose of the prescribed subject. For instance, history can no longer be taught as a subject requiring memorization of a plethora of dates and names. Students need to be made aware that the study of history is a prerequisite for understanding politics, social structure, and cultures.

When subjects are taught or learned in isolated compartments they rarely seem meaningful. Unfortunately most conventional schools still employ archaic linear and one-dimensional pedagogies resulting in students becoming alienated or disengaged from the learning process. When the only meaningful outcome of learning is a test or exam scores, students resort to mugging before exams and delete the information from their short term memory once tests are done with.

Multiple intelligences

The theory of multiple intelligences was put forth by Professor Howard Gardner in 1983. Professor Gardner is a Professor of Cognition and Education at the Harvard Graduate School of Education and was selected as one of the 100 most influential public intellectuals in 2008 by *Foreign Policy* and *Prospect* magazines. He believes that there are eight different types of intelligences. In order to understand what individual abilities and talents are, Gardner suggests that we need to look beyond just the intellectual capacity. People possess different intelligences, including musical, inter-personal, spatial, visual, and linguistic. A child may be exceptionally good at music

Type of Intelligence	What Smart	Characteristics	Career	Famous People
Visual spatial	Picture smart	Solving puzzles, using imagination, mind maps, drawing, painting, sculpting, good sense of direction	Illustrator, graphic designer, web designer, artist, sculptor, tour guide, cartographer, photographer, film director, interior decorator	Walt Disney, R.K. Laxman, Satyajit Ray, Mahesh Bhatt, Prahlad Kakkar
Kinaesthetic	Body smart	Sports, games, dance, hands-on approach, good hand-eye coordination	Dancer, sportsman, stunt person, racer, athlete, choreographer, soldier, fire fighter, policeman	Muhmmad Ali, P.T. Usha, Michael Jackson, Sachin Tendulkar
Interpersonal	Self smart	Good at talking to people, work well in teams, see other people's point of view, and have a large number of friends	Teacher, actor, marketing executive, policeman, salesman, doctor, nurse	Mahatma Gandhi, Martin Luther King, Princess Diana, Mother Teresa

Type of Intelligence	What Smart	Characteristics	Career	Famous People
Intrapersonal	People smart	Hardworking, can work on individual deadlines well, independent, prefer spending time alone	Detective, social worker, philanthropist, counsellor, writer	Claude Monet, Carl Yung, Sigmund Freud
Logical	Number smart	Puzzle solvers, ask questions, find logical patterns and sequences, problem solving	Accountant, book keeper, statistician, researcher, programmer	Thomas Edison, Albert Einstein, A.P.J. Abdul Kalam
Linguistic	Verbal smart	Reading, writing, debating, discussing	Blogger, journalist, author, poet, advertiser, copy writer, editor, radio or TV presenter	Charles Dickens, R.K. Narayan, Shobhaa Dé, Kushwant Singh
Naturalistic	Nature smart	Flourishes outdoors, Uses the sense of touch, smell and sound	Landscaper, gardener, biologist, animal trainer, chef, vet	Charles Darwin, Salim Ali, Sanjeev Kapoor
Musical	Music smart	Loves music, jingles, rhymes, rhythms	Dancer, musician, DJ, pianist, music director	Beethoven, Protima Bedi, Yesudas, A.R. Rahman

and painting but may not be so good at reading and writing. This does not make him any less intelligent than someone who can read and write but cannot draw and sing. Both have their own strengths.

Winston Churchill, Albert Einstein, and Thomas Edison all failed in school. Their learning styles was not suited to the style; in which they were being taught. Imagine how much poorer we would be if any of them had given up when the schools gave up on them.

Blooms taxonomy of thinking

Blooms taxonomy is a classification of thinking skills developed by Benjamin Bloom in 1956. He devides thinking skills into six levels moving from remembering to creating. The new emerging economy needs more people to have analytical and creative skills. The basic skills of needing to retain content or information or doing basic calculations are more or less done with the help of computers and search engines like Google. The skills of a human being now need to rise above the capability of machines.

Level (Lowest to highest)	Skills
Remembering	Describing, defining, labeling, listing, matching, omiting, memorizing, naming, recognizing, stating
Understanding	Classifying, demonstrating, illustrating, indicating, paraphrasing, summarizing, translating
Applying	Dramatizing, judging, calculating, implementing

Level (Lowest to highest)	Skills
Analyzing	Organizing, deconstructing, interrogating, comparing, differentiating, infering, surveying
Evaluating	Hypothesizing, appraising, defending, critiqueing, detecting, monitoring
Creating	Designing, planing, producing, devising

Most Indian schools still focus on the lowest level thinking skill—remembering. A few 'good schools' focus on the second lowest level thinking skill—understanding. Very few schools focus on the higher level thinking skills of creating and innovating. This is unfortunate because that is the future of success.

Coaching classes—to do or not to?

I have noticed that many parents in their eagerness to get kids admitted to good or reputed schools, enroll them in coaching classes, which claim to prep the child for admission to schools This is not required at all. Coaching classes turn a child into a parrot. This can be very dangerous as we limit the windows of opportunities to really learn.

When I began my first pre-school in 1993, every parent wanted me to get their toddler ready for entrance exams at reputed schools. I had to spend hours counselling parents on why that was not only a waste of time but would also stunt the true development of their child. I explained this to them with the help of examples such as the one below.

At birth, a newborn has poor vision. However, vision develops very rapidly in the first three years and continues to develop till the age of 7 or 8 years old. This period is called the window of opportunity for visual pathways to develop. If during this time the child develops a squint or needs glasses, his visual development may be delayed and, if not treated, may never reach its full potential. If vision is reduced and under-developed, it is called 'lazy-eye' or amblyopia.

Occlusion, or patching, is used to make a lazy eye work on its own and so improve the vision by encouraging the development of the nerve pathways from that eye to the brain. The patch is worn over the good eye and the amount of time the patch must be worn is decided by the orthoptist. If patching is implemented early on, good eyesight can be restored. However, if delayed beyond the right age, 8 in this instance, the window of opportunity for this development is largely closed since the age of development for the eye has already reached maturity.

I went on to explain that if I spend time making toddlers learn by rote for an entrance test—I would be doing a disservice to the child. My focus has to be on active learning instead and on maximizing all the windows of opportunity that are open.

Children learn from their surroundings. Therefore, active learning is very important. Restricting them to certain questions that enable admissions into schools is not advisable. Instead of opting for reputed schools, parents should look for a school that shares their values and makes the life of the student comfortable and stress free.

What does the child face today?

Kids today face the biggest contradiction of all times. They are expected to remember huge amounts of information for answering their papers, when they know that information is just a mouse click away. They don't see any meaning in retaining so much information except to score marks. Information storing, a left brained skill, is being done by machines. Then why do they have to do it?

The answer to this is something parents, teachers, and educationists need to arrive at soon, before we end up turning education into a purposeless, meaningless ritual. We need to realize that the value lies in the right brain, in the ability to ingeniously create using the resources available to us by the left brain expertise. Just as Steve Jobs once did.

The conceptual age is also about connecting dots or things that are seemingly unrelated. Steve Jobs also mentioned in his Stanford speech that life success is largely a matter of connecting dots. We go from one step to another, thinking that all the steps and incidents are stray cases. But it is not so. The dots somehow connect in the future. In retrospect they form a pretty neat pattern. That is why we have to trust that whatever occurs in our life is connected from the first dot to the last.

A reading of Rashmi Bansal's *Connect the Dots* shows the success stories of 20 entrepreneurs who succeeded because of their passion and their willingness to follow their heart. As we leave the information age behind, we need to guide our children to develop the aptitude and attitude required to discover their innate greatness. This type of success is not in tangible material comfort. It stems from the happiness that one experiences at a subconscious level and from being aspirational. Placing aspiration over ambition is a key value in my schools. We need to teach kids to aspire. As Prahlad Kakkar said to me, 'We need to add value to what we see. I may be cleaning a sofa, but how can I do it better than the others who are also doing it. When the value of 2 and 2 becomes 22 and doesn't remain 4, then we have added value to our life. The value of 2 and 2 as 22 has a great geometric proportion.'

I believe that the complexities of life are now increasing because of the rapidly changing business trends. Industry stakeholders are now demanding employees skilled in certain specific areas and resources that go beyond their subject knowledge or skill sets. It's not enough that you know your math or English well. You need to be a good communicator as well. Your role may ask you to empathize with people. A recent study shows that emotional reasoning is as important as the intelligence quotient in leadership roles. **The ability of a leader to take into account what his team members feel about things holds equal value in the industry today.** Brain research conducted on the best strategic planners of various companies showed that the emotional part of the brains worked at higher speeds than the intellectual part of the brain.

Such skills need to be nurtured harmonizing the energies of all three—the child, the parent, and the teacher.

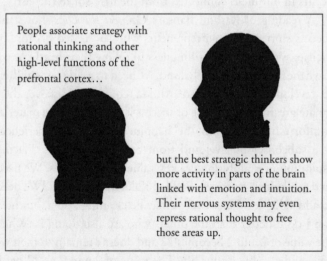

People associate strategy with rational thinking and other high-level functions of the prefrontal cortex...

but the best strategic thinkers show more activity in parts of the brain linked with emotion and intuition. Their nervous systems may even repress rational thought to free those areas up.

Source: Harvard Business review website

How can schools help children?

A child's requirements of knowledge, skills, and attitudes for success are different. As parents we must realize that what was good enough for us will not suffice for our children.

This is where schools can step in. Schools should now play a dual role—of educating kids as well as helping parents cope with the demands of a rapidly changing society. That is why I advocate that parents must be included actively and directly in the process of their kid's education. Schools need to provide parents necessary training and support to aid them in parenting. They should also help to develop parent awareness of physical and psychological needs of a child during different stages of growth. Workshops held by schools for parents to understand what their children need, in terms of mental, emotional, social, spiritual, and physical growth, will help create a successful triangle of the child, parent, and school. If parental involvement with children can go beyond just getting him to complete his homework or revising for tests, it will make our mission of providing education much more meaningful.

Every pre-school usually sees participation of parents in daily routine tasks. Parents volunteer for school projects, snack time, concert preparations, and emergency teaching. But our observation shows that as kids grow, parental involvement gradually decreases. More often than not, parental involvement in schools is limited to the PTA meetings or as audiences for annual days and sport days. If inclusive education is what we pledge to practice and if we really aim to tap into the innate greatness of every child, then why are we leaving out the parent? And this I believe is a serious omission. An adult usually has venues to proclaim his professional success. But where can he tap his potential as a parent? This can happen both at home and in school. Schools can become places where the parent is able to excel in the role he plays—that of a parent.

Does your child need to be a right brainer?

The 21st century doesn't demand only right brained or only left brained thinkers but whole brained thinkers who are ambidextrous in creative and rational thinking, having the courage to experiment with knowledge, information, as well as life at hand. I believe that our key responsibility is to oversee that the development of empathy in kids must accompany the development of logic and critical thinking ability. A child is expected to be a good team member and conform to the team's rules and regulations before expecting others to give him importance or prominence. He needs to be patient and agree to delayed gratification, be empathetic towards others, and understand what makes his friends and colleagues tick.

The future global economy is shifting to right brain capabilities that rely heavily upon ideas and creativity to solve the problems that the present day world offers. It is obvious, therefore, that we are shifting to a more abstract era where recognizing, understanding, and shaping concepts, trends, and the interconnectedness of the 'big picture' will serve us an important function. The development of such aptitudes relies more on innovative and unconventional education, which is counter to the familiar and rigid environments we commonly associate with learning in the classroom. Strict teachers, over populated classrooms, minimal student–teacher interaction, one-sided teaching approach with the focus on completion of the portion is what happens in a regular classroom. For the development of right brain skill sets, this atmosphere is the least conducive.

A career as a software engineer, finance analyst, and solicitor is still looked up to by Indian youth and their parents. As Indians are good at these left brain jobs and are cheaper to hire, these jobs are mostly outsourced to India from US, Japan, UK, Germany, and others. Pink observes this massive exodus of outsourcing of L-directed or left-brained white collar jobs to India in these lines:

'The programmers I met in Mumbai are but four well-educated drops in a global tsunami. Each year, India's colleges and universities produce about 350,000 engineering graduates. That's one reason that more than half of the Fortune 500 companies now outsource software work to India. For instance, about 48 percent of GE's software is developed in India. The company employs a whopping 20,000 people there. Hewlett-Packard employs several thousand software engineers in India. Siemens employs three thousand computer programmers in India and is moving another 15,000 such jobs overseas. And the list goes on. As the chief executive of GE India told London's *Financial Times*: "Any job that is English-based in markets such as the US, the UK, and Australia can be done in India. The only limit is your imagination.'

The fact is if mathematical, analytical, and mechanical skill-sets are primarily left brain skills and job prospects related to it are as bleak as above, then it makes sense to examine the increasing importance of right brain skills now in the current time. Thomas L. Friedman in *The World is Flat* (2005) observes why in the present time and space we must encourage our children to supplement high-tech abilities with aptitudes to see the 'big' picture, to detect patterns and opportunities, to craft a satisfying narrative, to understand the subtleties in human interaction, and find joy in oneself as well as elicit the same in others, and to stretch beyond the everyday commonplace pursuit of purpose and meaning to create a work of beauty so as to come up with inventions the world didn't know it was missing.

For me the 'big picture' not only involves what the commercial or financial world makes of it in terms of globalization or transcending regional and national barriers. The big picture is about the picture of life at large. It involves empowering our kids to set goals for themselves and help them follow a purpose in their life. It involves making children aware of the positive thought they are capable of; how their positive thought will help them do good not for themselves but for all around them and how the focus of life should be joy from within and not just without. It makes sense for present day Indian parents to nurture the right brain skills their children as the most urgent need of the day. Can we not make our children and youth aware of this fact?

Prahlad says that at his organization he finds it easier to hire the 'second class or pass class' students. This set of students he feels are the smartest. They are the ones who have discovered the shortest path to crack the boards. They know that they have to get a measly 35 percent to pass. They spend just that much time on studying. They realize that then they have enough time to do other things, making them more multi-faceted than the toppers. They have a hunger in them to prove things to the world that rejected them for so long. He says hiring toppers doesn't give him any benefit. He has to get them to unlearn what they have learnt and relearn what he needs from them.

So how do we then bring up children who are self aware and intelligent? Here are a few tools that are bound to help you in your journey:

1. The power of reading

Every period in history is defined by the tools invented in it and the way in which they were used. The definitions of the learner and the process of learning have changed. Education is no longer bound by the textbook, teacher or reference books in the library. The world of the student is open to the Internet. It is limited only by the child's ability and proficiency to read and learn.

The ability to read easily and proficiently is thus a skill all teachers and parents have to ensure children develop. It is only this skill which will ease children into self learning. Theories and methodologies regarding how to develop reading skills keep changing among educationists but there is unanimous agreement that practice is of prime importance to any reading programme. Differentiated reading strategies are important as different children have different learning styles.

Sight reading involves learning of new words as a whole and imprinting on the long term memory of the image of the word. If the child can see the picture of a ball and say it's a ball, show him the word ball five times and the sixth time he will read it as ball. Most kids can read McDonalds and Coca Cola way before they actually 'read'. This process develops the visual recognition of the reader so that he can become fluent with reading. Sight reading is a much more effective way of reading. Children who become proficient at it become speed readers. They also are more effective in 'reading for meaning' as their brain is not as burdened by decoding of the word in the brain and then attaching meaning to it. A good way to put this into action is to label most things in the house. TABLE. CHAIR. WINDOW. Have cards for the family that your child places on the dinner table. MUMMY. PAPA. DADI, PRERNA. PRATHAM.

Selecting appropriate books and making the stories exciting is of prime importance to stimulate reading habits. Therefore, choose a story you like to hear and then read it aloud a few times with good voice modulation to your child. You could whisper, scream, boo, and pause in appropriate places. Using your voice to complement the text and illustrations will bring the story to life.

My favourite novel is *The Alchemist* by Paulo Coelho. This book confirms my belief that there are no coincidences, only an universal design. The book is a masterpiece in symbolism. It tells the story of a boy who is in search of happiness, fulfilment, and the ultimate purpose of creation, and starts out on a journey to find it. Along the way, he learns to question these values and thoughts. At the story's end he discovers that the values he has been searching for, for so many years, lie in the journey itself. The story is a positive one with the message that you can get anything as long as you want it with all your heart.

One of the important ways we perceive our environment and our existence is by anticipating and telling ourselves stories. Making stories and adapting them to suit our environment and context is a strategy for making our world experiences and desires intelligible—a fundamental way of organizing or reorganizing relevant information.

The information we receive through stories then educates and influences our views and perceptions even if we try hard to avoid it. The fact is they are all part of our lives. Like metaphors, they seem to be everywhere. From fairytales and text book stories to the modern day novel, they always remain a part of our lives. Stories have been an integral part of human society. I attribute my positive spirit to the story of *Pollyanna,* a book I read as I underwent numerous leg operations. **The reason why stories are so powerful is that they engage the**

emotional centre of our brain. Most people can recall where they were when Indira Gandhi was assassinated or when Princess Diana died in the car crash. Most people will also be able to vividly recall their first kiss. These are the same people who may not remember what they ate for dinner two nights ago. We will remember parts of stories that resonate deeply within us.

Using a story as a spring board to learn is a great idea. Other than the conventional ideas of discussing characters and events, what parents and teachers can focus on are other aspects of learning derived from book reading. If a book is based on dreams, like *Peter's Dream* is, discuss the idea of dreams with the child: What is your dream in life? How do you think you are going to achieve it? What aspects of the story did you like the most? Have you at anytime felt disappointed like Peter did? How did you react then? Do you think you would react differently now that you have read the book?

Recommended Reading		
Ages	Book and Author	Summary
5 to 6	*Peter's Dream* by Dr James Hoffman	The book is based on the dreams of a little boy who escapes into a world where there are no restrictions on what he has to wear, eat, who his friends are or what routine he has to follow.
	Very Hungry Caterpillar by Eric Carle	With lots of holes for tiny fingers to explore, this interactive book teaches children about numbers, days of the week and time.

Recommended Reading		
Ages	Book and Author	Summary
	Cat in the Hat by Dr Seuss	By combining the funniest stories, craziest creatures and zaniest pictures with his unique blend of rhyme, rhythm and repetition, Dr Seuss helps children of all ages and abilities learn to read.
	Best Pet by Penny Matthews	Tom wants a pet he can play with. Monty the ferret is perfect. He's smart, he can run fast, and he loves playing hide-and-seek!
6 to 7	*Just Mabel* by Frieda Wishinsky	Just Mabel beautifully narrates the story of a young girl who is not happy with her name.
	The Owl who was Afraid of the Dark by Jill Tomlinson	This book provides the opportunity for emotional development in children.
	Judy Moody: Around the world in 8 ½ Days by Megan Mcdonald	Busy with her 'Around the class project', Judy learns about Italy with her best friends. Enter a new girl who is exactly like Judy and they form an immediate bond.
	Charlottes' Web by E.B. White	This is a tale of how a little girl named Fern, with the help of a friendly spider Charlotte, saves her pig Wilbur from the usual fate of nice fat little pigs.
7 to 8	*Charlie and the Chocolate Factory* by Roald Dahl	Charlie Bucket can't believe his luck when he finds a golden ticket and wins the trip of a lifetime around the famous chocolate factory.

Recommended Reading		
Ages	Book and Author	Summary
	James and the Giant Peach by Roald Dahl	Jame's aunts, Spiker and Sponge, beat him and starve him and make his life a misery. But one day he meets a mysterious man who gives him a bag of magic crocodile tongues and so begins the adventure of his dreams.
	Gulliver's Travels by Jonathan Swift	Gulliver gets washed up in Lilliput – a world filled with tiny people. Here begins the adventurous journey of Gulliver wherein from the world of tiny people he reaches the world of the giants. Though tumultuous it is a journey of great learning, discovery and victory.
8 to 9	*Matilda* by Roald Dahl	Matilda's parents have called her some terrible things. The truth is, she's a genius and they're the stupid ones. She gets the better of them and her spiteful headmistress, Miss Trunchbull, as well as discovering that she has a very special power.
	Harry Potter series by J.K.Rowling	Harry Potter thinks he is an ordinary boy – until he is rescued by a beetle-eyed giant of a man, enrolls at Hogwarts School of Witchcraft and Wizardry, learns to play Quidditch and does battle in a deadly duel. The Reason: Harry Potter is a Wizard!

Recommended Reading		
Ages	Book and Author	Summary
9 to 10	*The Eighteenth Emergency* by Betsy Byars	Mouse is understandably terrified when Marv Hammerman, the most feared boy in school, says he is out to get him. Mouse and his resourceful friend, Ezzie, are already armed with plans to tackle several horrendous happenings. The book deals with how kids survive classrooms and bullies.
	The Wonderful Wizard Of Oz by L. Frank Baum	When a cyclone hits Kansas, Dorothy and her little dog, Toto, are whisked away to the magical land of Oz. All alone in this strange world, they wonder how they'll ever get home.
10 to 11	*The Phantom Tollbooth* by Norton Juster	This book is all about appreciating the world around us. Through the example of Milo, a boy who is bored easily and can find nothing fruitful to do with his time, the author Norton Juster takes us through a book which is full of praise of the importance of education and the realization of self.
	Journey To The River Sea by Eva Ibbotson	Maia, an orphan, can't wait to start the long sea voyage where she is to begin a new life with relatives she has never met, a thousand miles up the Amazon river.

Recommended Reading		
Ages	Book and Author	Summary
	Tuck Everlasting By Natalie Babbit	Winnie Foster has everything a young woman could desire. But Winnie longs for freedom, for adventure. She escapes one morning to explore the woods surrounding her home, and encounters the Tucks, a close-knit family with a mysterious past that begs the question: If you could live forever, would you?

Contrary to popular belief, love of reading doesn't come naturally to children. Orville Prescott, principal daily book critic for *New York Times*, once said, 'Few children love books by themselves. Someone has to lure them to it. That someone is you.'

2. Encouragement

I remember my 3-year-old niece Anokhi once telling me as she cried into her bowl of corflakes, 'Lina foi, my brain just told me that I am stupid.'

A child's inner monologue does not just happen; it is born out of what they hear from other people. Children absorb words, feelings, actions, and beliefs from you and others and they internalize them. When kids hear good words, words of praise, and encouragement, they learn to respect themselves. They learn to praise the efforts of others too. If you criticize them over and over again, they feel ashamed of themselves. Kids will not be able to say anything positive about themselves unless they hear from us first.

Tell them to be mindful of the words they use, their actions, how they behave, and how they expect others to behave. Tell them you love them and are pleased with their good deeds. This will reinforce good behaviour and develop values.

Talking about having the right attitude and being positive is easier said than done. Research shows that we have almost 50,000 to 60,000 thoughts a day with over 90 percent being the same as the day before and almost 77 percent being negative. 'Most people keep thinking the same thoughts and visualize the same images in an unconscious, automatic manner. This means they keep viewing the same movie in their mind, and consequently, go on living the same kind of life.'[1] You can change the thoughts and images in your mind by changing the story in your mind.

It's not an easy job to keep your child motivated to think positively. But it is an essential part of parenting. Children have voices in their heads that tell them so many different and contrasting things. As parents, you should be able to teach them to look out for what messages their mind is sending them and how they can control it. One way to explain this to children is for them to view their mind as a garden. Each thought is a seed. This seed can be a weed seed or a beautiful flower seed. Doing so encourages children to be mindful of their thoughts. Another tip is to avoid the news till children are old enough to process the news. Everything we watch on television or read in the newspapers is specifically designed to stir up our emotions and put us in a state of irrationality and confusion. Even I as an adult only scan the newspaper for essential news and that too at the end of the day so my day's energy does not begin on a negative note.

Children also need a lot of encouragement to do their homework. Parents need to avoid falling into the trap of helping children with their homework for the sake of completing it. Then the homework becomes meaningless. Also, I always tell parents that the more you worry about homework, the less they will worry about it.

3. Positive thought

Mary Morrissey, an inspirational speaker, says, 'Doubts are like little worms that kind of worm their way in our minds.' We will either entertain our doubts and fears until they become the predominant force in our lives, or we send them away. We can make a choice to deny our doubts and instead turn our attention to our faith.

If we tell them that the world is full of ghosts and scary spirits they will develop an irrational fear of them. Instead, teaching them to be wary of strangers, not accepting rides or sweets from them or not accepting sweets from is prudent.

Get your children to say these over and over to themselves.

4. Taking their own decisions

Encourage kids to make small choices and decisions. These could be as simple as what clothes to wear or what shoes to buy. Motivate kids into doing the right thing by critiquing the action, not the child. Statements like 'you are a lovely child, you work so well, you have done a good job,' etc., help the child affirm the positive in him.

5. Teach your child to learn music

Music has a tremendous impact on memory and learning. It has been proven that children who study while Mozart is being played in the background have a higher activation of both the right and left brain. The information activates the left brain while the music activates the right brain.

Researchers at the University of Montreal used various brain imaging techniques to investigate brain activity during musical tasks and found that sight-reading musical scores, and playing music, both activate regions in all four of the cortex's lobes, and parts of the cerebellum are also activated during these tasks. Sergent, J., Zuck, E., Tenial, S., and MacDonall, B. (1992). 'Distributed neural network underlying musical sight reading and keyboard performance'.[1]

Kids may play music or sing just for themselves. They may be out of tune or not conform to the standard norms of music. But as parents we need to encourage them to explore it.

'Studying music encourages self-discipline and diligence, traits that carry over into intellectual pursuits and that lead to effective study and work habits. An association of music and math has, in fact, long been noted. Creating and performing music promotes self-expression and provides self-gratification while giving pleasure to others. In medicine, increasing published reports demonstrate that music has a healing effect on patients. For all these reasons, it deserves strong support in our educational system, along with the other arts, the sciences, and athletics.' Michael E. DeBakey, leading heart surgeon, Baylor College of Music.

In 1982, researchers from the University of North Texas performed a three-way test on postgraduate students to see if music could help in memorizing vocabulary words. The students were divided into three groups. Each group was given three tests—a pre-test, a post-test, and a test a week after the first two tests. All of the tests were identical. Group 1 was read the words with Handel's 'Water Music' in the background. They were also asked to imagine the words. Group 2 was read the same words also with Handel's 'Water Music' in the background. Group 2 was not asked to imagine the words. Group 3 was asked to read the words only without any background music, and was also not asked to imagine the words. The results from the first two tests showed that Group 1 and 2 had much better scores than Group 3. The results from the third test, a week later, showed that Group 1 performed much better than Group 2 or 3.

Introduce your child to various styles of music. Let your likes and dislikes of the various styles of music not limit you. Slowly he may just choose what suits him and his personality. Remember that anything forced will usually create resistance.

6. All round development

A polymath is a person of great and varied learning. His sphere of interaction has to transcend disciplines and have them culminate through interdisciplinary approaches to life. A polymath is someone who refuses to conform and will be difficult to tie down to one discipline or thought process. We need children who can break the mould and fly out to create a world for themselves.

Leonardo da Vinci was an artist, scientist, and inventor and each of his talents nourished the other in his work of art. Rabindranath Tagore, an artist, painter, composer, author, and singer is a rather polymath. Nathan Myhrvold, the co-founder of Intellectual Ventures, who earlier worked as the chief technological officer at Microsoft, is a prize winning nature and wildlife photographer. He also is a master French chef and is working on how to tackle global warming.

In this highly competitive job market such lateral thinking abilities are valued. If the child needs to branch out to explore

Surprise your Brain

I had an exercise expert tell me to start living life left-handed (since I'm right-handed) as much as possible. I was sceptical, but I've noticed that since I've been pulling luggage, lifting objects, and performing other everyday tasks with my left hand, my brain seems more receptive to learning other new skills as well.

For your child: In India, we have very severe cultural associations with the use of the left hand, for many it's considered impure. Break the mould. The use of the left hand activates the right part of the brain. Ask them to do the same thing to brush their teeth with the other hand, pick up their bags with their other hand. Simple tasks like that help the brain have cross references.

Embrace the unfamiliar: Don't listen to your favourite music for a while; try some totally different tunes. If you always read the sports page first, go for the business section instead. Since I have begun reading, varied material, I have noticed that my mind is ready to challenge itself to read and listen to different stuff.

For your child: Introduce him to a new art form. Get him a variety of books to read. Introduce him to a sport he may have thought he could play.

Change your schedule: Do not repeat the same schedule day after day. Once you break your physical schedule for the day, it just becomes easier to break your mental stagnation.

For your child: Children may need timetables at times but we can bring variety even in that. Have a different thing for breakfast. Experiment with cuisines for lunch or dinner. Rearrange furniture in their rooms. Reorganize wardrobes.

his other abilities and possess the mental agility to synthesize, to contribute new ideas, he needs to be given this option as a child. Expecting him to do so after he has grown into a conditioned adult will be asking too much of him. We need to ensure kids do not settle into a system of complacency that doesn't challenge their innate abilities. New ideas and breakthroughs will evolve only from free and horizontal cross thinking.

In order to initiate the process, let them participate in different activities that the school and community offer. They will find their passion eventually. Our responsibility is to encourage them to manage their time pragmatically and participate in different avenues. Open various avenues to them. Let them paint, dance, sing, play an instrument initially. Introduce one thing at a time. If they like something they will either want to do it or will let go. Do not make the task stressful.

7. Develop the skill of observation

Looking at life from other perspectives always offers opportunities to develop creative skills. The protagonist of Andy Andrews, best selling novella *Noticer* teaches a person to notice the small things of life, which enables them to make major shifts in their thinking process. Introduce the 'noticer project' to your kids. Play memory games with them. Keep many unreacted objects on a tray and give them a minute to observe. Remove the tray after the minute and them to inevite down everything they've fun.

Let us augment this creative alertness in our children. It's time to break the mould of the notoriously introverted, uncreative, humourless Indian.

Nurturning a personality

The Mahabharata tell us how Bharatha, after whom our country is named, had nine sons who were all rejected by him because they did not look like him! We inherit the way we look or the colour of our eyes and hair from our ancestors. That is a part of the DNA that we cannot escape. But do we inherit our tastes, our likes, and dislikes? Do we inherit our flair for writing or aptitude to play cricket? Can these be learnt? Yes it can be.

We need to wake up to the fact that we are not bound by our genes. We can do much more than that. Dr Bruce Lipton in his book *Biology of Belief* explains how the working of each cell in our body is affected by our thoughts.

Positive thoughts will be effective only when children are in harmony with their subconscious mind. All we need to do is to take a few simple steps to initiate our kids into programming themselves for success; success that will take them far beyond exams and grades.

The Transition Years: Tweens to Teens

The young always have the same problem—how to rebel and conform at the same time. They have now solved this by defying their parents and copying one another.

Quentin Crisp

It's not easy living in a war zone, which is what it usually feels like when there is a moody teenager to deal with. Things could be easier, however, if you knew the science behind why teens act the way they do. Remembering your own raging hormones and how atrocious your own behaviour was when you were 16 is comforting and helps deal with the temporary crisis. It can also help you and your teenager come out of it without any permanent battle scars.

But the questions remains: Why do teenagers want to push all our buttons all the time?

Teenagers have an emotional need to exert independence, push boundaries, and demonstrate their coming of age at every opportunity. This age is marked by rebellion and over-sensitivity. Tantrums one minute and tears the other. Your teenager herself is grappling with conflicting emotions—wanting intimacy with the family, but also the need to establish her own individual identity outside the family, for instance.

I was a tough teenager. I rebelled against every rule my father laid down, not just to assert myself as an individual, but to also question what I perceived to be archaic parenting. I ran twice as hard from what I thought was 'parental control' and yet I remember a time when my father said he only needed to know where I was in the evenings and nights, just in case I needed his help. I always told him where I was going after that and I used the same logic with my son, who as a teenager always informed me of his whereabouts. At some stage I feel my father evolved and decided that constantly fighting wasn't worth it. That sense of autonomy and control was what I needed at the time.

Traditionally, a teenager was someone between the ages of 13 and 18. However, in today's world, adolescence is setting in much earlier. And if you thought the terrible 2s were the only challenge, think again. The terrifying teenager is here to stay for the next decade. Because brain research shows that the brain rearranges itself significantly twice in a life time—once at the age of 2 and then again when the child hits his teens.

Tween

There is a new term for kids between the ages of 10 and 13.

We call them tweens.

This is a transitional phase and can sometimes be very frustrating for the parent as well as the child. They can feel the changes in them and are not sure whether they are still children, or adults. They want to be like adults, apply makeup, go out on dates just like their older siblings, but are at the same time restrained by their child-like impulses.

Tweens are usually very participative and active. Technology plays a very important role in their lives. They feel the need to be connected with their friends all the time.

How do I handle my tween?

'Janice has turned very rude. She snaps at anything and everything. The other day my husband just lifted her up as he usually does, she struggled out of his arms, screamed at him for doing this, and just ran away. Yesterday I bought her a lovely pair of clips but she refused to take them because they were pink. I always thought she liked pink! Overnight she doesn't,' Jean, 37, laments about her 11-year-old.

Tweens are little teenagers. Just as teens are confused about various things, so are tweens. We probably never experienced such a phase when we were growing up. But the situations are no longer the same. Early exposure to the world—from films and fashion to news from across the world—gives them an expensive view of life. They tend to fantasize about how things should be for them. They want to dress like the hottest film star. They want to ride on bikes and in cars that are high on the oomph factor. They want branded clothes, shoes, and accessories. Markets have been quick to notice that the growing distinctions between childhood ages are pronounced enough to warrant products, services, retail stores and marketing tactics specific to the 'tween' age group. Tweens are a huge consumer sector today. Couples with double incomes and young children seem to be spending a lot of money on this age group, more so to expedite their own guilt of not spending time with them. In India, market studies reveal that the tween is a more aware, demanding, and informed consumer and usually knows more about various consumer products than her parents.

'Nishit is just 11 years old. The first thing he reads in the newspaper are the prices of high-end cars, mobile phones, laptops, tablets, etc. He loves to collect information on discount schemes available on these products. He can rattle off the prices and the models of most of these products. His life today will be meaningful if he has a high end car, an android phone, a tablet. The television shows that he watches, the movies he sees, the newspapers he reads, all fuel his passion for such products. I cannot afford all this. How do I handle it without breaking his heart?' asks Adarsh, his father.

'Rishita told me that she had been invited to a party. I told her I would drop her to her friend's place and pick her up once the party was over. She agreed but requested that I not wear a sari when I went along with her. She told me that I was the only parent who wore a sari. She wanted me to come in a pair of jeans and T-shirt like the rest of her friends' moms,' said Neetu, a 45-year-old engineer.

Janice, Nishith, and Rishita are going through a typical tween stage. All three have begun to believe that they are more like adults. Tweens do not like kid treatments. They are not rebels without a cause, however, they just want to establish their independence, which sometimes involves being embarrassed by their own parents.

At this age, tweens are slowly discovering their inner potential and zoning in on their passions. Encourage them on this journey of discovery. It's not just about cuddling, cooing, and kissing. They now begin to have meaningful conversations. And they want you to respond to them in equally meaningful ways.

Janice stopped screaming and yelling once her parents gave her the due respect. They didn't treat her like a child. They did tell her how much they love her but without actually cuddling her. She was cuddled when she wanted it; not whenever they felt like it. When Adarsh recognized the other side of Nishith, his curiosity and his ability to collect information, he began to channelize his energies to help him set up a blog. Soon Nishith was blogging on cars, their engines and, of course, their rates and discounts.

'Harry barely has any time for me or the family. He refuses to come out with us on weekends and is happy playing cricket with his friends. He says he gets bored at family functions. I find it so difficult to get him to come anywhere with me,' says Rose, a teacher.

You will find that your baby is trying to move away from you. He is learning to see himself as an independent identity. He now realizes that he is separate from you, besides becoming aware of the way he is changing physically. What's most important for him now is his image in front of his friends; they are the focal point of a tween's life. He wouldn't like to be seen with his parents and family for too long at this point.

You'll also find your tween willing and able to answer back to you. She may not mean to be rude; it's just that her brain is developing and she may pose questions that sound like challenges to you or any other elder. She's still learning and not always mindful of the 'diplomatic' way of asking things. Which is why it is important that you reward her with praise when she speaks politely. Point out that rude talk reflects bad behaviour. At the same time, you need to model good behaviour. You can't yell at your tween but tell her not to do it. Simple steps like these will aid in meaningful communication between you and your tween:

- **Be patient:** There are bound to be arguments. Have patience. They are growing and will take time to understand what you are saying and why. Give them that time and space. Stand firm on appropriate behaviour.
- **Agree that he has a point of view:** Tweens have an opinion on everything that affects them. You may or may not agree. But give it your ear. If you agree, explain why you think he is right. If it's the other way, explain what you find amiss with his perspective. A dictatorial 'no' will not do.
- **Listen:** When he's trying to talk to you, put down everything else and listen.
- **Create talking moments:** Don't fix a formal time but set aside some 'talking time' whether it is at the dinner table or during a game of carrom after dinner. Chat with them. Discuss the best and worst part of the day with them. They will know that they can trust you and not hide anything from you.

The teenager

When we get our homes repainted or are refurnishing our offices, we encounter days of chaotic activity. The constant movement of workers in and out of these spaces can be disturbing. But when the home or office is finally ready, we enjoy the benefits of this newly developed space. This example can be used to describe adolescents. The brain is going through a makeover at this time and this disturbance is preparing your teenager for the next stage of life. He needs us to cooperate with him as far as possible.

Though they want to behave like adults, it is essential for us to realize that their disorganized brain has not matured and will not allow them to deal with things rationally like a mature adult brain would. They do not think when they are feeling and do not feel when they are thinking. Staying connected with what they want, think, and feel is important. When you find your teen behaving in a fashion that is not usually 'him', know that he is unable to cope with what's happening to him.

'I don't know what taken over Vicky. He wants to grow his hair long, pierce his ears, get a tattoo, and buy T-shirts which have the weirdest and craziest messages. He was never like that before. I am afraid he must have tried drinking and smoking too. He is locked up in his room all day. At times I feel I've completely lost my connect with him,' says Neena, Vicky's mom.

Vicky is going through a stage of transition. He is changing. And yes, he is at the stage where he wants to experiment. Talk *to* him not *at* him. This is an age when kids go crazy experimenting. They want to try new hairstyles, new clothes; because they want to fit in with the gang.

At this stage you need to understand what type of person your child is. Is he a leader or is he a follower? If he is a leader, the chances are that he is experimenting with new things only to find if they give him a 'kick'. He will find his own route. But if he is a follower, then you have reason to worry. He is not doing things because he wants to, but because others want him to. This is something you will have to watch out for.

Peer pressure

Peer pressure is at its highest at this age. Children want to fit in with their friends and look and sound 'cool'. They will face the pressure of taking decisions on their own, not wanting to sound uncool by having to take permission from their parents. These decisions could be minor ones like participating in a competition to serious ones like trying out drugs or cigarettes. Peer pressure has both positive and negative impacts. You may find him preparing for a topic to 'teach' his friends. But there may be times when they encourage him to try smoking or shoplifting. A few simple tips can help you teach your kids to handle peer pressure.

- Boost his confidence. Children who are not confident usually fall prey to peer pressure.
- Get to know your child's friends. So you will be able to know who they are mingling with.
- Encourage him to participate in volunteering camps, scouts, and guides camps, trekking expeditions and other positive activities. This will help them meet other positive minded children, which is bound to have a positive impact on their psyche.
- Listen to them. They may have valid reasons for what they are doing. Don't always lecture them.
- Teach children to say no. When they have the confidence to say no, they won't succumb to peer pressure.

Why is this transformation happening?

At this age, the bodies of children go through a sea change. There are changes that they can see and those they cannot. The bodily changes are visible and can be seen by the child. But the changing levels of hormones, like oestrogens and testosterone, trigger emotional responses from them.

Oestrogen stimulates growth of the womb and breasts and determines the shape of the female body. There is growth of pubic hair and girls begin to get their periods. In boys, the consequence of testosterone sculpt the body, increasing lean body mass and shaping features as well promoting body and facial hair. There is an increase in height and there may be a change in voice. The body resets the body clock. You will find kids sleeping later at night than usual and then waking up later in the day.

The sweat glands in the armpits and the groin areas are activated for the first time. Teach them to keep clean at all times. Glands in the skin of the face, shoulders, and back also become active at this time. Some children may find that their hair is oilier than ever. The nutritional demands of children at this stage also change. You will find that children at this age constantly hungry. This is the age when they can fall into the trap of junk food. Keep a watch. Ensure your home is stocked with fruits, nuts, and other nutritious food.

Different kids change differently. So your kid might suddenly look an adult or still look like a kid in front of his classmates.

These times are very confusing and trying. They need as much support from you as possible. Here are a few issues that could become conflict corners in your house:

- self image and body issues;
- eating disorders;
- choice of friends;

- virtual lives and Internet safety; and
- rebellion.

Let's understand why they behave the way they do.

The teenager brain is being rewired at this stage. Two important things happen at this point—one is the creation of new synapses and pruning of older ones. Pruning is the process of eliminating unused synapses in the brain to help it to function more efficiently. **Synaptic pruning is thought to help the brain make the transition from being a child to an adult.** The other is a process called *myelination.* The neurons in the brain are 'nude' till now. A white fatty tissue called myelin begins to cover them. This tissue increases the speed of transmission of information.

The region where maximum pruning takes place is in the prefrontal cortex, the part right behind the forehead. This area is responsible for sophisticated thinking abilities, planning, and weighing risks and rewards. This part matures only by the late twenties. This is why teenagers are very high risk takers and love to experiment with new stuff. Their brain does not tell them what could go wrong! This area of the brain is also involved with the feelings of empathy and higher order thinking skills. MRI scans of adults and teenagers have shown that though both groups use the same part of the brain to handle similar situation, the activity in the brain of a teenager is very less compared to an adult.

Teenagers are also unable to multi-task. This is because the part of the brain that multi-tasks has not yet developed. So multiple commands confuse them.

Most teenagers are pleasure seeking. They enjoy their music, food, clothes, and friends because they are fun. They are loud and noisy because it gives them pleasure. This is because the brain releases a chemical called dopamine, which is responsible for the feeling of pleasure. **The release of dopamine is at its highest during adolescence.** Their quest for pleasure, if threatened by the adult world, will result in rebellion. This causes the child to be motivated by short term risks.

In a recent study, scientists found that the adolescent brain is extra sensitive to the rewarding signals it gets when something goes better than expected. The discovery might help explain why teens take risks—from driving too fast to experimenting with drugs—that don't seem worth its while to adults because they are unable to perceive the long term hazards. They get a 'kick' out of speeding, experimenting with cigarettes, drinks, drugs, and anything that the parent says is forbidden. The thrill of risking one's self outweighs the dangers at this time. Adolescents are uniquely sensitive to the uncertainty in the world. Their willingness to engage in uncertainty is driven by the potential rewards that might result from that uncertainty. For them, the rewards are much bigger than the potential negatives.

Self image and body issues

The life of a teen is not easy. Teens usually have serious self image problems. The media devotes so much time and energy on projecting the perfect man and the perfect woman that children begin to feel inadequate. They feel awkward, isolated, and highly conscious of how they look. Societal acceptance of their looks is very important in their lives. It is a paradox that the teenager rebels and at the same time wants to be accepted by his society! Many teens have issues handling their own bodies. Anything and everything becomes an issue. Height, weight, hair colour, its length, spectacles, dental braces, clothes, school bags, stationery, almost anything becomes a part of the self image. The presence or absence of any one of the above could add to the problem.

Sometimes as parents our expectations of how children should look also causes a lot of stress. Statements like 'Why do you grow your hair?', 'Do you have to have such long nails?' 'Oh God! You got your nose pierced!' could conflict with their self image.

Empower your child with a strong self image, which will help him love himself for what he is. Speak to him. Tell him what the media portrays in not always the truth.

Encourage him to exercise. Simple household tips to fitness will help. Slices of lime in a litre of drinking water will flush out his toxins and give him the clear, pimple free skin that he craves for rather than the chemical combinations available in the market.

Teach them to dress according to their body shape. They need not fit into the tightest of clothes. They should just be comfortable in their clothes. Comfort will exude confidence.

A positive calm and peaceful atmosphere at home, which aims at conveying to kids that they are loved as they are, will give them the confidence to face the world.

Open Pathways	Closed Pathways
What do you think?	You are too young to understand.
That's a good question.	You don't need to know that. Don't ever ask me that again.
I don't know, but I will find out.	Why are you asking me that?
Do you want to talk about it?	That's none of your business. Why do you need to know that?
Do you need any help?	Don't come to me if you mess up things.

How to Talk to a Teen

- Use a positive tone. If you are sarcastic and rude, your teen will not want to talk to you.
- Eye contact is essential. He will know he can trust you.
- Use open gestures. Avoid pointing fingers. Open your arms. Let them know their conversation is welcome.
- Hug and kiss your child. It works at any age.
- Keep your smile in place when talking to your teen.
- Stop what you are doing. Listen to what your teen wants to say.

Eating disorders

Rathi is 13 years old. She has a secret. And the secret is affecting her daily life. She can't control herself from eating junk. She knows that these are unhealthy, nevertheless she enjoys them too much to not have them every day. But after eating them she throws up. This began almost a year ago. Rathi gained weight and soon found her friends teasing her for it. She did not know how to lose it so she began to force herself to vomit what she ate. This became a habit and today she knows she cannot control her urge to eat junk food.

Devang is 17. Living in a family that loves its food, he is very conscious of how much he eats, more so because he is mortally scared of gaining weight. He eats as little as possible. He exercises really hard. Today he is gaunt and thin but at most times feels tired, sleepy, and sick. He also complains of frequent stomach aches.

A huge issue that stares in the face of parents is the eating habits of their teenagers. While there is a media generated frenzy for the perfect body on the one hand, there are large varieties of junk food alluring them on the other. Thus, they either eat all the wrong foods or nothing at all, which can lead to dangerous eating disorders such as bulimia and anorexia.

Bulimia is a state where the child eats too much food and is unable to control his food intake. But in order to ensure that he doesn't gain weight by this unhealthy eating, he vomits the food out immediately after eating or uses laxatives to ensure weight loss. Anorexia is trying to limit the amount of food consumed so as to ensure that there is no weight gain.

Initially people thought that only teenage girls suffered from eating disorders, but research has proved otherwise. Eating disorders stem from wrong eating patterns, eating the wrong type of food, and eating too much or too little. The culprit behind these disorders is a lack of confidence or the absence of a positive self image.

A self-confident child will not have a negative self image and will not put himself through these dangerous situations. Watch out if you feel your child is obsessing about how much he/she is eating. Be aware of their eating patterns. Research shows that people with eating disorders have very low levels of two neurotransmitters—serotonin and norepinephrine—both responsible for the emotional well being of the child. Serotonin also helps manage information in the brain. Thus, children who have eating disorders are usually hazy and do not connect the dots as smoothly as they otherwise would.

Teach your kids the benefits of eating nutritious food. A healthy lifestyle will give them the comfort of being confident in their skin and they will not resort to unhealthy, life threatening tactics just to keep up their self image. Healthy food does not have to be boring food. Discuss the foods they like to eat and have a menu planned for them. Change this weekly so that they get to eat all types of food. Ensure that every type of food from the food pyramid is covered in the menu. Take popular food like burgers, pastas, and rolls, and make them at home instead, with your own healthy twist. That way you ensure that your teenager does not crave it outside.

Choice of friends

'But, Ma! Raj is my best friend! He understands me. You guys don't. He is the only one who knows what I need, how I feel and what I think. You want me to do what *you* want!

Parents and teenagers are usually at loggerheads over the friends a child keeps. While some parents are chilled out about who their child's friends are, others get very anxious.

Teenagers begin to look at peers as their support. They have now moved out of the ambit of the parent and want to explore everything. This begins with friendships. Some friendships that they make during this period last a lifetime. Look into your own life. How many of your friends are still with you today? As we grow up, we have made our choices about our friends. Trust your child to do the same.

This is an age when children want to experiment. This experimentation goes on to choosing friends also. Soon they will filter their friends.

A few but important things you should make a habit of:

- call their friends home or go out for picnics. Arrange parties for them. But let them alone. Do not hover around like a helicopter;
- get to know the names of his friends. Discuss with them why their friends are important;
- get to know his friends. Your concern may just not be justified;
- don't go by appearances. Children want to experiment at this age. His friends are also experimenting with their clothing;
- tell your child you trust his choices;
- respect his friends and you will win them over; and
- trust yourself and your upbringing. Remember, when you do not trust your teenager, you don't trust the values you instilled in him.

'I let Fahad do what he wants. I invite his friends over. I have discussions with him over the guys I am not comfortable with. But he only seems to get angry with me. I thought by being a friend, I have him with me. No! I still don't. Where am I going wrong?' asks Raheena, 47, a seamstress.

Even after doing all that needs to be done, if your child is still withdrawn, it indicates a sense of loneliness in him. He lacks self-confidence. Talk to him. Find out where the vacuum in his life is. If required, get a third person he trusts to talk to him.

The teenage years are also a reflection of what the subconscious mind imbibes during the growing stages. Whether a teenager is comfortable in his skin or not has a lot to do with how he has grown up. A traumatic childhood affects the teenager's mind. As the teenager moves out of the home and meets new people, the brain goes through a constant state of wiring and re-wiring. But this happens on the basic subconscious template that has formed through childhood.

Thus, as a parent, if we ensured that the mind template supplied to them positive and happy, one can rest assured that the age of experimentation will pass soon. Your children will come out of the tumultuous teen ages triumphantly.

Virtual lives and Internet safety

The Internet is a vast resource, a storehouse of information. But it is also a warehouse of hazards. Even simple key word searches can lead them to dangerous places on the net.

Just type 'how to' on Google and you'll discover that the most searched for things include 'how to kiss' and 'how to get pregnant'! The doorway is open and the threats are imminent.

Awareness about the dangers of the Internet is essential. Children are as vulnerable to Internet strangers as they are to real life ones. Chat rooms, social networking sites, gaming zones are all areas where children can meet unknown people. People can take them into confidence and violate their privacy. Children will not always or immediately realize what is happening to them.

As I have discussed earlier, children love to experiment during this time. Making online friends is also a part of their experimentation. There is a lot of sexual content online and their laptop, tablet, and iPad can provide them a platform to view such content within the confines of their room. Sexual content is a topic of high interest for kids this age and they may be motivated to probe further.

Watch out for signs that your child may not be using the Internet for productive reasons:

- the child spends long hours on the computer, especially at night;
- he changes the screen the minute he sees an adult around; and
- he is withdrawn from the family and wants to spend time online.

Teach them Internet safety. Social networking sites are important but also guide them about what they post on their status. Corporates today are looking up social networking sites to gauge the value systems of a person. So a photograph of the child smoking or revelling in a drunken party may sound like bravado today, but can lead to adverse consequences in the future.

The virtual world is also an attack on your privacy. Teach children to keep as much information private as possible. Tell them that at no cost should they reveal full addresses, phone numbers, or family information.

The world is moving towards technological connectivity. All devices are connected through a cloud, a Drop Box, or Google docs. These help connect your mobile, laptop, tablet, and puts all of them on a virtual sharing platform. Information input in one device can be used in another device. This constant connectivity can become a noose that gets tighter and tighter.

My child is a rebel!

'Archana, clean up your room!'

'No, mom. Let it be...I can find my things. Why bother?'

'Archana, I cannot have you live in a dump like this. Clear it up right now!'

'No, mom! It's my dump. Why are you getting irritated? Chill. And call me Archie…'

'You are Archana and you will clean your room NOW!'

Archana aka Archie slams her door and stays put inside.

'I am losing it with Archana. She rebels over everything. Her name, clothes, attitude. Everything! I am always wrong. I can't imagine why. I would never have spoken to my mother like that. But does she care? Why is she like this?' Mamta, a 39-year-old doctor, worries about her teenager.

I explained to a hysterical Mamta that Archie is just being a teenager. But more importantly she is a teenager of today. The world we have given them is different from what we got from our parents. And the world they will be taking over when they are adults will be different from what we believe it will be. Try to understand why they are rebelling against, or more importantly, what they're trying to tell you. A teenage rebel, as long as he is not hurting himself or anyone else in the process, is someone you can encourage. At an age when most teens want to fall in with their peers, if yours is able to stand his ground, you should appreciate it. Sometimes might is right, and it takes strength of character to stand up against the world. **You should know that the more you try to curb the rebel, the more you're fuelling him.** So be careful about the limits you impose and what you ask him not to do. A better way is to open up a dialogue and discuss the subject in question. More often than not, rebellion is a way of asserting independence. You know you craved for it when you were his age. Let your teenager indulge in it too.

Brain research has proved that the emotional aspects of the personality develop in the brain before the rational part and that is why a teenager is so high on emotion. Logical, rational arguments, too, at times don't work because the brain processes only the emotional aspects of a conflict. This also explains teenage mood swings.

As they move from tweens to teens, the regions in the brain responsible for logic are better connected with those for emotional reasoning. Thus, you will notice that as they grow, they are able to handle their emotions better.

Instilling habits of gratitude

My son Drish and I once went to my aunt Tina's house for her son Anmol's birthday party. On our way back I noticed that 3-year-old Drish was sulking.

'What happened, sweetheart? I asked.

'Anmol's bathroom is bigger than my bedroom. You know, ma, he has an entire aquarium in it,' moaned Drish.

I carried him in my arms and asked him a simple question. 'Who do you think has a bigger bedroom, Raj or you?' Raj was Drish's closest friend and Drish often stayed over at his place.

'Me!' said Drish, with a twinkle in his eye.

'Okay, and between Raj and Gungun?' I asked. Gungun was a little girl who lived down the street in a two BHK.

'Raj!' he said.

And then I asked him about Krishna, our watchman's son.

'Ma, Krishna has only one room in his house. They don't have a bedroom!'

'Right, but who do you think is happier, Krishna or that little fellow who begs at the signal?'

Drish was quiet. Then he slowly answered, 'Ma, I think Krishna must be happier. He has a room to stay in. The beggar boy sleeps on the footpath.'

'Yes, my dear, now you see how much you have. Shouldn't you be thankful that you have so much more than the others? If you look at what you have, you will be happy. If you look at what you don't have, you will only feel low and disappointed.'

Children today find themselves in a world of abundance. They get almost everything they want. Being grateful for what we have ensures a positive attitude towards lives. Positivity and happiness are the keys to a successful life. It has been scientifically proven that positivity and happiness hold the key to a healthy life too. A research done by Perreau-Link and colleagues, research scientists at the National Centre for Biotechnological Information, USA, published in the *Journal of Psychiatry and Medicine*, that changes in the thought process, either aided by someone or self induced, alter the synthesis of serotonin in the brain. Serotonin, as I mentioned earlier, is the hormone that manages the happiness quotient in a person. So this research almost proves that there is a give and take between the amount of serotonin produced and the mood that we find ourselves in. A good mood means more serotonin, which, in turn, means a happier and healthier person. A foul mood logically leads to less serotonin and an unhappy and unhealthy person.

Sexuality

Sex education is an important part of adolescent education. This is the time when children acquire information and form their attitudes and beliefs about sex, sexual identity, relationships, and intimacy. Sex education is important so that children are able to make informed choices. This will help them stay away from teenage pregnancies, HIV, AIDS and other sexually transmitted diseases, sexual abuse, and exploitation.

They should be able to identify other's behaviour towards them and be prepared to thwart any sexual advances.

Children need to have the information and skills to handle a topic like sex. At the pre-adolescent and adolescent stages, sex usually has a tinge of mystery and romance. Life is beautiful when someone of the opposite sex is attracted to you and the teenager will feels the need to impress the person he/she likes. And here is where the child faces the contradiction.

Ira, a 16-year-old, once came up to me to talk about her troubles because she was too embarrassed to broach the subject before her parents. 'I like Raj and I know he likes me. We are good friends and are being called a couple by our friends. We go out for movies and lunches. He comes home and I visit his house too. Our parents know each other and have met on a few occasions. The other day he tried to kiss me. I was upset. I was not sure if that was right. If I let him do that, would one thing lead to another? Was I prepared for that? I am working hard in school and want a good career. But this incident has made me moody and irritable. Raj is upset because he thinks I am angry with him. Why am I so confused?'

The media portrays romance as the most beautiful thing in life with couples running around trees, singing songs of undying love, even willing to end their lives if their love is rejected. On the other hand, news and information about child sexual abuse is rampant that children find these contradictions slightly difficult to perceive.

Sex education, thus, is an important life skill that we need to pass on to our children. It gives them the reasons as to why people have sex. It lets them think about the emotions involved, respect for oneself and one's beliefs, respect for other people and their beliefs, and the choice to make their decisions. It teaches them how to identify the positive and negative aspects

Sex Education

Parents need to be comfortable speaking about sex to their children. Assess your own value systems first. Increase your level of comfort with the topic. Discuss with professionals or read up about the topic. Garner support from other parents if you need.

- **Sexual development:** Talk to them about the changes that happen in the body during puberty.
- **Reproduction:** This topic is almost taboo in our country. Explain the process to them. They need clarity not vague references as shown in the movies.
- **Contraception and birth control:** Safe sex practices need to be encouraged to avoid sexually transmitted diseases and unwanted pregnancies.
- **Love and commitment:** Focus on relationships and love as the base for a happy sex life.
- **Cultural and religious connotations:** Talk to them about how your culture and religion views it and how you feel about that in your family.

of the relationships they share. It helps them foster love and reject abuse.

Rather than trying to scare children from having sex and scarring them for life, having open discussions about sex and its implications benefit the child. There are many published fiction and non-fiction books to assist you with this process. *Boys, Girls & Body Science: A First Book about Facts of Life* by Meg Hickling provides no-nonsense answers for children, and parents. Specifically designed for young readers, *Boys, Girls & Body Science* walks children through the wonders of their bodies in a direct, easy-to-read manner. *It's Not the Stork! A Book About Girls, Boys, Babies, Bodies, Families and Friends* by Robie H. Harris. *Just for Boys* by Matt Crossick and *Just for Girls* by Sarah Delmage are just a few that you can refer to.

Child sexual abuse

Child sexual abuse is rampant, and today's child needs more preparation than ever. Most parents are usually in a state of denial. 'This cannot happen to my child.'

But the sad truth is that it can happen to any child. One of the most distrubing types of child abuse is sexual abuse. This happens far more often than we would like to believe. The surprising fact is that it is the most well kept secret in many a family. We would rather believe that it doesn't exist than talk about it and find a solution to it. Talk to your child about this. No child is too young to be warned. In fact, this needs to begin as soon as the child is around 2 or 3 years. Teach the child the difference between good touch and bad touch when they are infants.

As they grow older, teach them what constitutes child sexual abuse.

Tell them that no one can:

- touch their private parts;
- tell them to touch other people's private parts;
- show them sexually inappropriate material;
- fondle, kiss or touch them on their lips or their private parts; and
- force themselves on them.

It is important for children to know that they need to be safe and that one can learn to be safe. Child molesters are usually people known to their victims. It is because the child knows the adult that allows the adult to do what he is doing. Most victims have agreed that their molester was a person either related to them or well known to their parents. **Research shows that 89 percent of the victims know their abuser.** They abuser is usually a part of the family or someone close to the family. The incidents of child sexual abuse can take a heavy toll on the child. Research also shows that the perpetuators of crime are usually victims of abuse themselves. And that is not something we would like to accumulate in the subconscious bank of the child.

A child going through sexual abuse may at times not tell you out rightly but he will try to reach out to you. Keep yourself open to the signals. A child is usually taught to obey his adults. So he doesn't know if what's happening with him is right or wrong. The reluctance to speak out against an adult and the fear that the adult may retaliate harshly may make the child keep quiet.

'I was 10 years old when I was touched in the wrong way by my uncle. Initially I did not realize what he was doing. But then it made me uncomfortable. I told my mother about it but she laughed it away saying that "Mama (uncle) loves you and its okay." Soon this took a dangerous tone and I was abused by him till I was almost 15. That's when I decided to throw a tantrum in front of everyone present. Since that day he hasn't stepped into my house,' says Rani, a victim of child sexual abuse.

Keep your ears and eyes open and most importantly believe your child.

Sex education can happen in the formal school structure and the informal family setting. Both are essential. Parents are well placed in the informal family settings to have such kinds of discussion based on what and when they want to speak to the children. The important thing is to initiate discussions on this topic at home and make the family comfortable dealing with the topic of sex and sexual relationships.

The tweens and the teens are notorious for their tumultuous years. But you can sail through this age with fewer hiccups if you are able to maintain a positive attitude towards whatever is going on in their lives. If the children are happy in their tweens and teens, research indicates that they turn into positive, happy adults. Researchers from North Western University also found that teens with high positive well being had a reduced risk of engaging in unhealthy behaviour such as smoking, binge drinking, using drugs, and eating unhealthy food as they transition into adulthood.

The Exam Years

I was thrown out of college for cheating on the metaphysics exam; I looked into the soul of the boy sitting next to me.

Woody Allen

Dheeraj is very jittery. His exams are due to begin in another couple of days and despite all the preparation, he is still unable to remember all he has learnt. His mind just seems to shut down the moment he sees a question paper. He is petrified of what he will do once he is in the exam hall and also worried about facing his father after every paper. He feels he will let down the family 'name'. He feels he will not do as well as his brother who topped his class.

He jumps out of the balcony of the fifteenth floor and ends his life. It seemed like the easier option for him.

According to National Crimes Records Bureau, in the years 2008, 2009, and 2010 the number of people committing suicides due to failure in examinations was 2189, 2010, and 2479 respectively.

Why have exams become such a big stumbling block for children? Why are exams snuffing out lives? Can we even visualize the amount of pressure that we are putting our children through?

The teenage years are definitely exam years in India. Class 10, 12, and the umpteen number of entrance exams, rule the life of a teenager. But do we need to make these years as painful as we did for Dheeraj and the thousands of others who chose to end their lives before or after exams?

A positive approach and some hand holding will do a lot of good for an entire generation. Simple steps can make exams less traumatic. As a parent, you can help your child with:

- goal setting and motivation; and
- charting out what they want to do.

Goal setting

As a parent how many of us actually sit with the child to brain storm what he/she wants to do in life? Most children do not know why they are studying what they are studying. The main issue with children today is the lack of guidance vis à vis goal setting.

As they grow into teenagers, children begin to have ideas about what they want to do in life. These ideas need to be analysed and put down as focussed goals.

The brain has a system called the Reticular Activation System (RAS). This system works like a filter choosing what is to be sent to the brain for processing and what to filter out. The brain uses visual clues to decide what information to retain and what to discard. Through the day we experience multiple inputs of data, but we pick only the ones we need. This is because we set the filters in our brain according to what we need. The best thing about this system is that the filters can change as and when we need them to. A filter is set once we focus on something, not otherwise.

The RAS is activated by 'programming' goals into our subconscious mind which acts as the power centre. This mechanism thus explains why goal setting is such a scientific principle. The brain is like a computer; waiting for instructions. The brain and the subconscious are neutral. They will listen to what you feed in. Thus, goal setting goes a long way in helping the brain focus. Once the goals are set, the brain sets the filter in such a way that it accepts only what it needs. So we need to ensure that the brain sets positive filters.

If your child is struggling with math, set a simple goal of doing ten problems a day. Ask your child to think positively about the whole exercise. The moment the brain says, 'I have to do ten problems a day', math will no longer seem like a battle which must be won.

Dheeraj had turned on all the negative filters in his mind by worrying about his father's response to his already assumed poor performance, the anxiety of results, and the pressure of the family's expectations.

Goal setting is an essential step in the process of achieving success. It is the road map telling your brain which direction you need to head towards. This is a habit that needs to be created in children because they cannot at the age of 15 suddenly be expected to know what they want if they have never thought about it before.

If you have not yet discussed your child's goals with her, do it now. It's never too late to begin.

Begin with basic tasks when your child is about 4. At this age, her goals can be as basic as 'Today I will brush my teeth well' or 'Today I will help mom clean the sink'. As they grow older, they can be assigned more complex goals. When children become tweens and teenagers, motivate them to frame their own goals. Goals could range from getting good scores in the exams to buying an iPad.

Break the goals into smaller steps

We are all familiar with the concept of setting SMART goals: goals that are Specific, Measurable, Attainable, Result Oriented, and Time Oriented.

However, I find this happening at a very materialistic level for most people. Goals should not only change the outside world of a person in terms of possessions and material comfort; the most powerful transformation is the one that occurs within. There is a saying: "'How does one become a butterfly?" she asked. "You must want to fly so much that you are willing to give up being a caterpillar.'"

Life is all about growing and transforming, and the story of the journey from a caterpillar to a butterfly is the universe's reminder of the importance of change.

True happiness and success is attained when one reaches one's 'peak state' physically, emotionally, spiritually, and cognitively. I encourage children to believe that each one of us must everyday take baby steps towards our peak state. As we evolve our potential peak state shifts and evolves with us.

Goals should not just be framed to attain more money or luxuries, but should be framed to help us transform our children from within. These inner goals find their essence deep in the subconscious mind of the individual.

For me the definition of SMART is different.

Your goals should find their orientation from the *Subconscious*.

Goals should *Motivate* you.

Goals should mould your *Attitude*.

Goals should *Reverberate* your personality.

Goals should be *Tangible*.

Subconscious orientation

Krishna is 22 years old. He is a part of the football team representing his office in an international tournament. He remembers the time when he was 14 and was unsure of what he wanted to do after Class 10. He had always been a good football player but his parents could not see him making a successful career out of it and encouraged him to do other things. Krishna, however, was adamant and wanted to do a language course in college, which would leave him with enough time to focus on his football. He also did his groundwork on colleges, which offered the best facilities for football. Raji, his mom, however, was very sceptical and wanted him to pursue his engineering and go abroad for higher studies. Because he could not convince her of his choice of subjects, he had to bend to her wishes and began his engineering classes. Of course, he found no purpose in them. Things changed when a new football coach joined his college. His involvement in football increased and things began to change. Motivated by his coach, he began to practise football seriously; he was so happy and satisfied with his performance on the field that he was motivated enough to concentrate on his academics too. Soon he began to represent the college in national and international football matches. He owes his present job to his success in football. 'Finally, it was passion that rescued me,' he says. 'If I had not got the chance then, I was sure that I would've quit engineering to allow football to take centre stage in my life.'

Children as young as 15 are expected to make important career decisions, which are bound to affect them for their entire lives. How sensitive are we to what they desire and what they need? More often than not, goals for children are set by the parents. We decide their subject choices, their careers, and almost everything else about their lives. We fail to realize that their failures and successes have a subconscious undercurrent. When they choose what they want to do, they find more positive energy to do it. With the power to decide a course of action comes the responsibility of fulfilling it. When children are equal participants in the decision making, they feel responsible for their decision.

Motivation

Goals will motivate only if they have a sense of purpose to the child. When the child sees no purpose in a routine and finds no happiness in achieving something, he is not motivated to do it. Just like Krishna was attending engineering classes for his mom and not for himself, most kids withdraw from a routine as it does not serve any purpose. Motivation will bring in persistence and ultimately lead to success.

Thomas Alva Edison said, 'I have not failed. I have found 10,000 ways that don't work.' Edison, singly and jointly, holds a record of 1093 patents. He had to have a very intense level of intrinsic engagement to persist through the 10,000 ways that did not work.

Discuss the goals set with your child

1. Are they important for him?
2. Does he see any meaning in pursuing them?
3. Does he believe he can achieve them?
4. Is he setting them to please himself?
5. Is he setting them to please his friends or parents?

If he has a 'YES!' for the first four, then he is surely motivated by his goal. Motivation will lead to persistence and focus. But if question number five is also answered with a 'YES!', then the chances of him being happy and successful are bleak.

Attitude

Lalit is an intelligent boy. He wants to be a pilot but lacks the passion to achieve what he wants. He is very laid back and unfocussed. This lackadaisical attitude is not letting him achieve his dreams. Lalit and his father sat down and listed his goals. They went through the process of defining his long term goals as well as his short term and daily goals. But it was not until he really decided to work on the goals that things changed for him. He needed an attitudinal shift to get him to begin his work. As he began to surmount the smaller goals, he realized that he could do what he had set out to. His belief in himself and his goals began to gain strength.

Michael Jordan on Goal Setting

The famous basketball player Michael Jordan said in his book *I Can't Accept Not Trying: Michael Jordan on the Pursuit of Excellence*:

'When I got cut from the varsity team as a sophomore in high school, I learned something. I knew I never wanted to feel that bad again... So I set a goal of becoming a starter on the varsity... When it happened, I set another goal, a reasonable, manageable goal that I could realistically achieve if I worked hard enough... As I reached those goals, they built on one another. I gained a little confidence every time I came through. ...If (your goal is to become a doctor)... and you're getting Cs in biology then the first thing you have to do is get Bs in biology and then As.'

Goals should also help children develop the right attitude and approach to life. Attitude is created by our beliefs and mindsets. So these also find their base in the subconscious of the child. When goals are set, they will need the right attitude and belief systems within them to sustain them through the journey.

Reverberate your personality

Once the attitude has taken shape, maintaining it will help the child to reverberate his personality. This will help your child develop confidence. The habits of gratitude (see pX) and maintaining a positive approach will cause a resonance of energies. A meaningful combination of the energies in the child will help him to chart out his goals better. Teach your children the following simple tips to keep their energy levels high:

- exercise;
- eat nutritious food;
- read inspirational stories. For example, Sudha Chandran, a successful actress and dancer today, lost one of her legs in an accident when she was in college. Sheer grit and determination has helped her reach where she is today;
- laugh long and loud;
- celebrate every success, even if it is a tiny one. Celebrate a debate prize or even a painting done well;
- be kind to someone you don't know. Donate a pair of shoes you are not using to the orphanage; and
- avoid comparing yourself with others in the class. This adds to stress. Go at your own pace.

Tangible goals

Goals that are tangible can be converted into reality. They need to be seen, written, and felt. Simple tasks like asking children to visualize their final report card can work wonders. Ask them to write out small tasks that need to be completed and keep them pinned on their study tables.

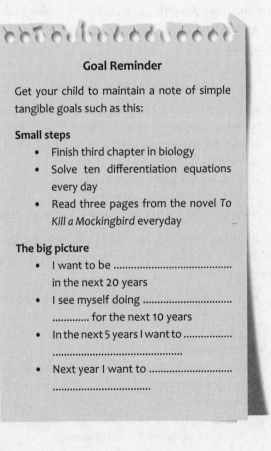

Goal Reminder

Get your child to maintain a note of simple tangible goals such as this:

Small steps
- Finish third chapter in biology
- Solve ten differentiation equations every day
- Read three pages from the novel *To Kill a Mockingbird* everyday

The big picture
- I want to be ....
  in the next 20 years
- I see myself doing ....
  .... for the next 10 years
- In the next 5 years I want to ....
  ....
- Next year I want to ....
  ....

Intangible benefits

While focusing on the tangible, children should also be taught how to be mindful of the intangible. The intangible benefits of maintaining tangible goals are many. Point out to your child how much time he has saved while sticking to a plan. Discuss with him how his skills of working and time management are getting better by the day. As they achieve each goal, they will realize that they have the potential to do things successfully. With success will come the happiness and pride of achieving bigger goals.

Recognize Stress in Your Child

- Is your child sleeping too much or too little?
- Is there a reversal in the sleep pattern?
- Is your child missing his classes?
- Is he feeling isolated?
- Is he not spending time with friends?
- Is there a change in his food habits?
- Is he participating in too many activities to avoid studying?

If your answers to more than five of these are yes, then you should know that your child is stressed out and you need to help him alleviate it.

- Encourage your child to get enough sleep. Help him set a pattern.
- Ensure his food habits have the proper nutrition required for him to study.
- Let him participate in some form of exercise. Encourage him to play some badminton or tennis. Swimming once a day can also help.
- Encourage him to spend time with his friends, watch a movie, or meet up for lunch or dinner.

Academic plan

The exam years have to be personalized like a tour programme. Once the goals are listed out, jot down the actions that can be taken to achieve the goals. The exams are usually in the months of March to August. Preparation for these begins at least a year in advance.

Swathi is calm and composed even though her board exams are beginning tomorrow. This is because she had made a time table for herself and she stuck to it. She is well prepared and in a happy frame of mind.

But next door, Sunita is a mess. She had spent the last few days with her cousins who had come from the US. Now she just has the night to revise 14 chapters, 15 poems, *and* a Shakespearean play. She plans to stay up the whole night. Her mother is worried she may fall asleep while writing the paper tomorrow.

The difference between Swathi and Sunita was their approach and their treatment of the challenge that lay in front of them. Swathi was planned and had worked out everything right down to the last detail. This systematic approach to the exams helped her keep stress away.

Plan out the year for your child. Break down the syllabi into months, even weeks. Tackle each topic independently. The child should be comfortable and familiar with the syllabi by the time the exams draw near. His performance has to peak at the right time or he will suffer from severe stress and anxiety when the exams come around.

How to plan?

- Create a monthly timetable for your child.
- Discuss with him the topics that have been studied in every subject.

- Match the revision schedule to suit the pace in school. Many parents have the habit of wanting to complete three or four cycles of revision before the exams. This may clash with what's happening in school.
- Get your child to use smart study techniques like the use of graphic organizers or SQ3R.
- Arrange the books according to the set timetable. You will not waste time hunting for books or pencil boxes if you organize your study table before retiring to bed.
- Monitor the child's performance in tests.
- Look for any changes in interest or energy levels.
- Ensure that your academic plan has enough time for relaxation and fun too.

Chart your progress

Do a weekly review of the portion set out. Tackle extra assignments and projects in the beginning of the year so that they don't pile up by the end of the year, right before the exam.

The chart gives a weekly/daily break up. This helps children plan their week.

Work out the daily blocks with your child. Figure out what time slot works for them to study, for revision, for play, and for homework. Accordingly, slot their time. The blocks I have given here are for one hour. These can be broken into half hour slots or rearranged into 50-minute slots, depending on how long your child is able to concentrate. Remember, every child is different and what works for one may not work for another.

Planning the day does not mean being rigid and dictatorial about them. These schedules will need to include time for play and fun. The adage 'all work and no play makes Jack a dull boy'

Time	Sunday	Monday	Tuesday	Wednesday	Thursday	Friday	Saturday
Morning till noon							
6.30–7.30							
7.30–8.30							
8.30–9.30							
9.30–10.30							
10.30–11.30							
11.30–12.30							
Noon till night							
12.30–1.30							
1.30–2.30							
2.30–3.30							
3.30–4.30							
4.30–5.30							
5.30–6.30							
6.30–7.30							
7.30–8.30							
8.30–9.30							

has a lot of truth in it. Children need to refresh their minds if they have to work hard.

Food plan

Children at times get so immersed in their work that they forget to eat! As children move into college they get dependant on coffee or cigarettes to help them keep awake through the night while studying or working on projects. Such things also ward off hunger and make children develop various deficiencies that make them tired and withdrawn.

Food is the source of energy for the mind and eating the right type of food is essential. Most children succumb to eating fast food due to two main reasons—the easy availability of such products and the lack of time to prepare good food. Simple dietary changes are the key to enabling higher levels of concentration in the children. A few points to keep in mind:

- ensure that their diet is rich in fruits and vegetables;
- keep them off junk food. It makes them lazy and lethargic;
- several mini meals through the day work better than very heavy meals at longer intervals;
- encourage them to drink water. Children often neglect drinking water; and
- healthy soups, fresh lime juice, and other fresh fruit juices should keep their energy levels positive and high.

Plan almost everything else

Distractions are galore. Friends, television, games, pets, emails, messages, Facebook updates, and lethargy—the list is endless. These are an essential part of student life but children can be motivated to put in shorter, but more concentrated hours of study, as opposed to distracted longer ones. Talk to your child and help him map out his best practices. A few points to keep in mind:

- let your child figure out the best place for him to sit and study undisturbed;
- ensure the place is well lit and ventilated;
- let your child put up a Do Not Disturb sign if required. The rest of the family may not want to put all their activities on hold for the time he is studying. So if your child is going to use a room that his siblings share with him, ensure that the siblings have taken whatever they need from their room for the time he wants to use it undisturbed;
- if music works for them, let them play it in the background;
- figure out if your child is a morning lark or a night owl. Let him study at the time he finds convenient;
- set a routine. The body and mind usually get into a smooth flow if put in a routine. This will help them focus better;
- add incentives. Get his friends to do group study sessions. Send them for a walk or treat them to some ice cream. Though small, these motivational tricks are of significant value;
- ensure they change the subject they are studying every hour and a half. Monotony can kill enthusiasm. If fatigue sets in, the brain cannot function optimally; and
- walk and study, sit and study, stand and study. Keep changing the way children place themselves.

Develop good study practices

1. **Encourage them to be in the present**: If they are thinking of a match they will not be able to focus on what they

are mading. At times it helps to give children a dose of distraction so that the mind is able to concentrate on what it wants to focus on. So if they want to watch a match... it's okay. But once the match is over, they will have to train their minds to be in the present and focus on the task that needs to be done.

2. **Give your child time out**: Ask your child to note down what troubles him. Take time out to discuss his issues with him. This activates the Reticular Activation System (RAS). The brain knows that this is the time to focus on other issues and sort them out. Once the issues are sorted out, the brain reallocates the filters to then focus on tasks at hand.

3. **Let him visualize concepts**: Draw mental pictures of how current flows through a conductor or how the Battle of Versailles took place. These will help him remember what his studying better.

Is coaching essential?

Jayant, 42, a father of a Class 10 student said to me, 'Colleges are demanding almost 100 percent marks for admission. My child should score at least 97 percent if he has to stand a chance. I enrolled him in extra coaching classes in Class 8 so that both of us don't have to face the music later on. Even before he has completed Class 9, the coaching classes have begun with the Class 10 syllabus. By the time of the Board exams, they will have repeated the syllabus at least three times. I am sure my son will do well.'

My personal belief is that all coaching classes should be banned. The future belongs to 'open book exams' and access to Google where the focus is not on retaining the information but in application of that information. Further, we need to create a balanced scorecard that scores for aptitude as well as attitude. I am worried about some of the teenagers I encounter. Many of them score in the 90s and above but are rigid in their thought process, don't have social interaction skills, lack confidence and self-esteem, and have no sense of a larger life purpose. Many of them have the information and the formulae, but no 'functional' use of the information.

Most parents believe that enrolment in good coaching will help their child max the board exams. Parents pay exorbitant amounts for the classes. Reservations of seats for these classes begin almost a year in advance. The growth of these coaching classes is a scathing indictment of our education system. The fact that everyone is looking outside the school to ensure academic success reflects the state our schools are in. The lack of quality teachers and their inability to attend to each of the 50 to 70 students in every class compounds the movement towards coaching classes.

Veena, 39, a mother of a Class 10 student says, 'We live in a nuclear family. With both of us working, my daughter, Vinita, is a latch key child. I prefer she goes to extra classes as there is someone monitoring her time in the second half of the day. The other thing is, I don't understand math and physics. How am I to guide her? At least I know there is an expert guiding her a coaching centre. Her time is controlled and she is doing something worthwhile.'

For many parents, coaching classes are necessary evils. This stems from the fact that with both the parents working out of home, they are not able to devote as much time as they would ideally like to. Not only do coaching classes act as babysitters during the time the parents are unavailable, they also help to regulate and manage the time of the child. Many

parents also feel that at this age, teens may listen more to a teacher than to them.

The exam years can be handled with minimal stress and maximum pleasure if they are planned well. Optimum planning ensures that both the child and the parent have a smooth ride through a bumpy road!

Career Choices

You are not here merely to make a living. You are here in order to enable the world to live more amply, with greater vision, with a finer spirit of hope and achievement. You are here to enrich the world, and you impoverish yourself if you forget that errand.

Woodrow Wilson

Sylvester Stallone was an attendant at a food counter before he became a movie star. From writing in cafés to becoming a multi-millionaire J.K. Rowling traversed through difficult times. Mahatma Gandhi went from being a lawyer to a freedom fighter. In more recent times, Chetan Bhagat quit his career as an investment banker to become a writer. Devdutt Pattanaik worked in the field of pharmacy and healthcare till he gave it up to become India's most renowned writer of mythology.

This chapter brings us back to where we began. We began by looking at parenting, education, brain research, and their implications on our children as we realized that the world was looking at more competent people to run it. From here on you need to address your child as an adult as he is now ready to take his own decisions in life.

So by now, you should be able to identify what type of learner your child is, what his strengths are, and what he should focus on to find a career that suits his personality. Going by what Daniel Pink said, 'If we are going to rule the world, then our children need to have more well suited careers to choose from. A degree is an added benefit, but it no longer guarantees a job.'

Think of a career, not just a job

A job, as defined by the Oxford dictionary, is a task or piece for work for which one is paid.

A career, on the other hand, is an occupation undertaken for a significant period of a person's life with opportunities for progress.

The key words here are surely 'significant period of time' and 'opportunities for progress'. This is what distinguishes a career from a job. A career should be something that is able to sustain a person's interest for a significant period of time and challenge them to learn, enabling progress through life.

For ages, Indians have happily lived with the idea that a person is 'settled' if he gets a job. This craving for stability has driven Indian parents to motivate children to get into careers that offer job stability. The sense of being financially secure was given the highest priority. This had a lot to do with the economic standing of the country at that point of time. Post independence, engineers, doctors, and administrators grew as the nation began building itself.

The scenario has changed today. Markets have opened up and globalization has placed a multitude of options before our children. They have the means and the right to experiment. A career has to be one that suits the person's attitude and aptitude. It should not merely be to 'settle' in the conventional sense.

Which career to choose: My choice or my child's?

The board exams are just the beginning of the journey. The number of career options are increasing. This is where parents play a crucial role in helping children decide what they want to do. Most parents want their children to follow the dreams of the parents. Parental pressure to choose careers is very high in our country. The traditional mindset of the child doing what the father or the mother does is very strong. This stems from our history. During the Vedic time, we had the varna systems where children were born into professions. The son of a brahmin was always a brahmin or a priest. The son of a king became a king, the son of a cobbler became a cobbler. This system seems to be coming back into our society where engineers, for example, want their sons or daughters to be engineers. We see families of doctors and businessmen. Universities are conducting management programmes on how to run family businesses. Children who want to step out of this system are looked upon as anomalies.

A friend of mine inherited a company from his father. The business was not running well and he spent his whole life trying to resurrect it. But his talent lay in painting. After he inherited the business, he has not made a single painting. Our country lost out on one more M.F. Hussain because of the family pressure of having to run a flagging business.

If you don't want this happening to your child, give him the choice to decide his career path. It is after all his life. There are a number of counselling centres that run aptitude tests. You could ask your child to go to one of those if you feel that it will give you a better picture, but my suggestion would be to let your child follow his heart. I recently read a statement on a church board which said: 'The heart may be on the left side, but it is always right. Listen to it.'

I agree. Let your child follow his dreams.

What to think of before deciding on a career?

Riva's mom came to meet me, upset and distraught. Riva had got a seat at a medical college which was giving her a substantial scholarship.

'Then what's the issue?' I asked.

'Riva! She doesn't want to go to a medical college. She has also cleared her entrance for architecture and wants to go there. How do I get her to go to medical college?'

'What would you prefer, Mrs Mehta, an A grade architect or a C grade doctor?' I asked.

Once you get that answer, your dilemma will be sorted out.

Chart the path ahead

Once the exam results are out, and the initial sense of relief has passed, it dawns on children that they have to take life-defining decisions. Choosing a college major or the course of education will decide the next few years of their lives. And most children and parents hit the panic button at this time!

The key is to not panic. Simple self analysis tools will help answer these questions. Ask your child to answer the following questions:

- What do you see yourself doing happily 10 years from now?
- What preparation will you need for that?
- How will you prepare?
- How do you see yourself different from your peers?
- What is that one thing that you really, really want to do?
- What are the skills you need to be successful in your chosen field?
- Are you equipped with those?
- Are there courses you could do that would equip you with them?
- Do your values and beliefs find compliance in the college you have chosen?
- Collect brochures and read up about colleges and how they function online.
- Get a reality check! Are you sure you want to be a doctor or are you doing it only because your father is one?

What interests your child?

You wouldn't want him to be trapped in a career that does not suit him. Let him decide what his interests are. List them down. Prioritize them. Let him decide what needs are to be satisfied immediately. Observe your child. You will be able to recognize where his aptitude lies.

- **Does the option offer him a sense of purpose?** Just as learning should have a sense of purpose, the career should also have one. Is the career option giving him a sense of purpose? Is it giving him a sense of direction?

- **Is he optimistic about the prospects?** Is his mind flooded with optimism when he speaks to others about his plans? Is he enthusiastic about it? Is he raring to go?

- **Is he ready to work hard?** No career can thrive based only on interest. The initiative to work hard is necessary for success. Is he ready to work as hard as the career demands?

When the above questions have been answered, he will be able to decide what career he wants to embark on.

How to approach his/her career?

Your child is now moving out of the safe cocoon of school or college and entering the big bad adult world. The first step in this world can be daunting. But all it takes is a positive approach and open mind to tackle this problem. Encourage him to:

- dream big but have a plan of action chalked out to help him attain this dream;
- take small steps. He may flounder and fall but if he is focused about what he wants, he will be able to achieve it;

What to do when your child doesn't know what to do?

There are times when a child might be confused about his interests or career choices. Do the following with your child:

- Make a list of what careers he thinks he wants to pursue. Ask him to list them in descending order of choice.
- Decide the pros and cons of the top three. If he wants to become a heart specialist, in the pros put down that he cares for people. In the cons put down that it takes almost 10 years for the career to finally take off.
- List out what he needs to make the career:
  o What training does he need?
  o Which colleges offer it?
  o If not college, then what other courses do you think he would need?
  o Does his option require specialized training?
  o Where are these offered?
  o How much income will you generate through your options?
  o Is money an important factor?

- keep a positive attitude. The mind achieves what it believes. So if his attitude is negative, it will be self defeating. In any circumstance, he should be able to keep his mind upright and positive; and
- be sure about what he wants to do. Once he is self-confident, the world will play along with him.

Dare to dream

Dream small! Dream big! Dream any way! A big dream is only a combination of smaller dreams. So let children stick to their dreams and watch them unfold with time. The following steps should be able to help them achieve their dreams:

- list out their dreams. Encourage them to choose the dream that arouses their passion to do something;
- approach the dream with what they want to learn and what they want to earn. Initially, the earning may be lesser than the learning but in the long run, it will be profitable;
- take small steps. Ensure progress over small periods of time;
- make adversity a teacher. Everything that goes wrong teaches a new lesson;
- trust their instincts and thoughts when it comes to their dreams;
- let them be unreasonable and demanding with their dreams. It will motivate them to go ahead; and
- let them hold fast to their dreams. They will turn into reality one day.

Get lucky

Luck is not coincidental. It can be invited into our life. Richard Wiseman, professor of Public Understanding of Psychology at the University of Hertfordshire in the UK, conducted a study which proved that those who think they are unlucky should change their outlook and discover how to generate good fortune. He believes that people are lucky when they are able to spot opportunities for success in life. In his book *The Luck Factor*, he has put down a few techniques for us to draw luck into our lives. They are:

- create and notice chance opportunities in your life;
- listen to your intuition. Think and feel about situations. Your gut feelings may just act as an alarm to rethink and reconsider decisions;
- create self-fulfilling prophecies with positive expectations;
- adopt a never-say-die attitude that will turn the tide;
- avoid becoming victims of routine. Variety is surely the spice of life; and
- see the positive even in the negative.

Upgrade

The changing and demanding dynamics of the markets will not allow for any complacency to set in. Upgradation in life is a must and parents need to inculcate the idea of change into their children. The suggestions I have given here are applicable to both.

- Read…at three levels. The first is for entertainment, the next is for professional growth, and the third for personal growth;
- pick up a new hobby. This will challenge and entertain you;
- set up an exercise routine. A healthy body is essential for any success;
- challenge yourself. This could be in any way. Learn a new language, lose weight, write a book;
- acknowledge that you are happy in what you are doing. No one is perfect. Only then will you be able to move ahead and progress;
- acknowledge your flaws. You may or may not spend time on working on them. But you cannot ignore them;

- let go of the past. Negative emotions from the past can tie you down. Let them go. Forget and forgive people who have wronged you. Heal yourself and move ahead; and
- take a break. Rejuvenate yourself. You will work better.

Change is inevitable

Any job that is not based on the inner calling is never the final destination. Authors like John Grisham and Robin Cook were in different professions before they switched to writing. Grisham was a lawyer while Cook was a doctor. They converted their experiences into novels. Daniel Pink himself was a law student who was writing speeches for other people till he decided to become the author of his own work.

Children may experiment with regular jobs just to learn how things work and may want to venture out on their own. It is this change that we need to accept because after all, change is the only constant.

Ready to Go

There are only two lasting bequests we can hope to give our children. One is roots; the other wings.

Hodding Carter

I had a builder send his younger son to one of my pre-schools, while his older son went to some other school. A year later, he withdrew his son from my school without any reason. I met him one day and asked him why he had taken his child out of the school. He said, 'My son is getting too cocky. He asks questions about everything. If I ask him to go to bed, he wants to know why. If I ask him to do anything, he questions me.' I smiled and thought to myself, 'That's a thinking child you have there.' But what he told me next was what rattled me. 'If I can't control him now, how will I be able to control him when he grows up?'

Many people thought I was a mean and irresponsible mom for allowing Drish to travel to Singapore alone at the age of 4. My older brother Hiten was waiting for him there to take him to Australia. Drish and I used to travel together regularly from when he was 3 months to the age of 4. He filled up his own forms (even though I had to do them again!) and lugged around his own hand baggage. People were aghast. I had to explain myself to everyone that I believed there was no correct age for him to do anything. The correct age was and is when he is ready. His physical safety was a given. He would fly as an unaccompanied minor on Qantas. I only had to be concerned with his emotional safety. We talked it through numerous times, preparing him for his journey. How will you feel when the air hostess takes your hand away from my hand? How will you feel and what will you do when you want to go to the toilet? I knew by his answers that he was ready. The next time Drish and I were about to get on a plane to Australia he beseeched me to take another aircraft. When I explained to him that I could not do so, he pleaded: 'Okay, Mumma, can you at least sit in another part of the plane?'

I know of mothers and fathers, who don't know how to give their children the emotional and physical space that they need to develop confidence, independence, and a separate sense of self. They volunteer at school everyday to be closer to their children. Many adults have never resolved their own dependency issues, and transfer their dependency on their parents or partner to their children. They failed to become self-reliant and now are unable to foster independence in their children.

To ensure that the child is emotionally strong, the parent has to be so in the first place. When the parent is strong, the children are able to leave their homes as strong, confident individuals who make the right decisions and abide by them. Guiding our children to be strong people emotionally is one of the main roles of a parent. When we parent in this way, our children learn to base their own relationships on these principles. Only when we are strong and independent can we develop nourishing and fruitful relationships with others. If the parent is weak emotionally, and is dependant outside of himself for emotional security, he will find it very difficult to provide the emotional stability for his child.

Parental control

In India, parental control over their childrens' lives is very high. This has a lot to do with the culture that we belong to. Respect and obedience are virtues that are sworn by. But the problem arises when these turn into instruments of control.

Legally, a child turns into an adult at the age of 18. He can vote for his parliamentary representative. But isn't it surprising that at one end of the spectrum, the government thinks 18-year-olds are old enough to choose their representatives, but parents feel they are not old enough to choose their careers or life partners? Parents need to realize that once children have grown into adults they have the right to take their own decisions and be responsible for them. Unless they are allowed to make their own decisions they will never learn to take up responsibility. Many parents think that solving their child's problems is their duty. But if we make their problems ours, they avoid taking up the issues themselves and avoid responsibility.

'It's her new job. How can I not go with her? I will drop her to office every day,' says Hariharan, 60, father of 22-year-old Nandini. Nandini is a working adult, but is still treated like a child in kindergarten.

'I have been working since I was 22 years old and my parents expect me to hand over my entire salary to them. My father invests the money. He says it is for my future. I am given a monthly stipend from the salary I earn. If I speak to them about how irritating it is to live as if I were still in college, they get upset. They say I don't trust them with my money or that I will end up spending all the money I earn. The irony is that I work as a financial planner and here I don't have the right to invest my own money. Their investments will all mature 20 years from now. By then I will be too old to execute plans that I have for myself now. How do I explain to them that I have a life, that I am an adult? I need my independence,' complains Atul, 27, who works as a financial planner.

'Everyone in my office is going for an overnight picnic. But my parents will not allow me. They believe that it is not safe for girls to go on trips. It is very frustrating and embarrassing,' says 25-year-old Niti who works as a marketing executive.

Once they are adults, we need to realize that they now want their own space and time and we have to let go of them. This process can be emotionally draining if you are not prepared for it. But the preparation to let go should happen even as children reach Class 7 or 8.

My parenting philosophy finds deep resonance with Kahlil Gibran, the author of *The Prophet*.

> Your children are not your children.
> They are the sons and daughters of Life's longing for itself.
> They come through you but not from you,
> And though they are with you yet they belong not to you.
> You may give them your love but not your thoughts,
> For they have their own thoughts.
> You may house their bodies but not their souls,
> For their souls dwell in the house of tomorrow,
> which you cannot visit, not even in your dreams.
> You may strive to be like them,
> but seek not to make them like you.
> For life goes not backward nor tarries with yesterday.
> You are the bows from which your children
> as living arrows are sent forth.
> The archer sees the mark upon the path of the infinite,
> and He bends you with His might
> that His arrows may go swift and far.
> Let your bending in the archer's hand be for gladness;
> For even as He loves the arrow that flies,
> so He loves also the bow that is stable.

You have invested almost two decades in your child. Know that your time and energy have been well invested. Let your child soar into the world as a strong, self-sufficient individual.

Redefine the empty nest syndrome

This is a stage in a parent's life when the children have left home to lead their own lives. Parents usually feel depressed and lost during this stage. After having spent so much time with their children, parents suffer an emotional upheaval on letting them go. This is when the parents should look towards remodelling their own lives and not become victims of the empty nest syndrome. Remember how you prepared for the first day of pre-school? Similarly, prepare yourself for the time your child leaves home.

If you know your child will leave next year, begin to plan what you will do once he has left. But if your child leaves home suddenly, do not panic. Only if you are calm will he feel confident to move out. Your confidence in him will increase his self-confidence. If your child feels lost initially, you may want to feel happy that your kid cannot do without you, but you should encourage him to find his place on his own. It will teach him to be strong and independent.

Decide ways to keep in touch with your kids. With mobile phones and emails, connectivity is no longer an issue. At times, you may want to know what's happening every minute of his life. You may be tempted to call or text too often. Avoid this. Keep communication lines easy and pleasant. Do not turn into a remote control parent.

Shift the focus. Traditionally, we have been conditioned to run our families till we have the energy to do so. But now is the time to relax. Do all that you have always wanted to do for yourself. Take a vacation. Rediscover the romance in your marriage. Go on a long trip with friends. You don't need to worry about exams, bruised knees, or pancakes for breakfast. Register for a university course. Conduct a course. Embark on the career you had abandoned because you wanted to take care of your children.

As Harry Emerson Fosdick, an American pastor, said, 'Don't simply retire from something; have something to retire to.'

Plan your time as much as you plan your finances. You are more than a parent. Discover the inner you and find a new identity.

Find a hobby that inspires you. Write, draw, paint, sing, carve. Go ahead and do things that you have always wanted to do.

The options are endless. Always remember to be prudent and, most importantly, to follow your heart.

Notes

Chapter 1

1. Children, Adolescents, and Advertising, The American Academy of Pediatrics. American Paediatric Association in December, 2006 (Vol. 118 No. 6, pp 2583–2589)
2. Intrinsic Motivation, Theroux,P. http://www.davidsongifted. org/db/Articles_id_10648.aspx

Chapter 2

1. Blog: IBOSOCIAL, Darren Sanford. http://www.ibosocial. com/itmakesscents/blog.aspx?blogid=110587
2. Empathy Causes Facial Similarity Between Couples To Grow Over Time, Jeremy Dean. http://www.spring.org.uk/2007/07/ facial-similarity-between-couples.php
3. Why Actions are Preceded by Past Programming, Burt Goldman. http://www.quantumjumping.com/blog/why-actions-are-preceded-by-past-programing/
4. 22 Powerful Tools to Transfer Your Fear Into Happiness, Peace, and Inspiration, Iain, Cyndi, Phil, Jeff and the Evolution Team. http://www.scribd.com/doc/43015757/Powerful-Tools-to-Transform-Your-Fear
5. 22 Powerful Tools to Transfer Your Fear Into Happiness, Peace and Inspiration, Iain, Cyndi, Phil, Jeff and the Evolution Team.

http://www.scribd.com/doc/43015757/Powerful-Tools-to-Transform-Your-Fear

Chapter 3

1. You got emotionally hijacked, now what?, Jorge Estrada. http://www.progressivedairy.com/index.php?option=com_content&view=article&id=8804:you-got-emotionally-hijacked-now-what&catid=49:management&Itemid=75

2. Introduction to The Winner's Brain, Jeff Brown and Mark Fenske with Liz Neporent. http://thewinnersbrainbook.com/excerpt.html

3. If Your Goal Is Success, Don't Consult These Gurus, Lawrence Tbak. http://www.amquix.info/yale_goal_study.html

4. Using Logical Consequences. Exchange Press Inc. http://www.childcareexchange.com/eed/news_print.php?news_id=3136

5. Using Logical Consequences. Exchange Press Inc. http://www.childcareexchange.com/eed/news_print.php?news_id=3136

6. Life kills Development/Module Four/entrepreneurship. Wiki Educator. http://wikieducator.org/Life_Skills_Development/Module_ Four/entrepreneurship

7. Enterprise Education. Department of Education, Employment and Workplace Relations, Australian Government. http://www.deewr.gov.au/Schooling/Programs/Pages/vocational_education_enterprise_education.aspx

Chapter 5

1. http://www.askmen.com/dating/single_fathers_400/491_father-to-friend.html#ixzz26yuECjUq

2. http://www.sarahbesthealth.com/healing-father-daughter-relationship/

3. Like Mother, Like Daughter, Stef Daniel. http://www.

professorshouse.com/Family/Children/Articles/Like-Mother,-Like-Daughter/

4. 'Twixt Ma and Religion, Madhu Jain. http://www.outlookindia.com/printarticle.aspx?231306

5. Oedipus Complex, David Straker. http://changingminds.org/disciplines/psychoanalysis/concepts/oedipus_complex.htm

6. The importance of a mother in a son's life, Melissa Murphy. http://www.helium.com/items/1884990-what-influence-does-a-mother-have-on-her-son

Chapter 7

1. How Food Affects Your Moods, Elaine Magee. http://www.medicinenet.com/script/main/art.asp?articlekey=56719

2. How Food Affects Your Moods, Elaine Magee. http://www.medicinenet.com/script/main/art.asp?articlekey=56719

3. Baby Einsteins: Not So Smart After All, Alice Park. http://www.time.com/time/health/article/0,8599,1650352,00.html

4. Toddlers. About.com Pediatrics. http://pediatrics.about.com/od/toddlers/a/05_terrble_twos.html

Chapter 8

1. *Why Right Brainers Will Rule the World*, Daniel Pink: 2005, pp. 49–50.

Chapter 9

1. *Science*, 257, 106–109.

2. Becoming the Boss of the Mind, Remez Sasson. http://www.successconsciousness.com/index_00001a.htm

Acknowledgements

I thank Random House for allowing me a voice, and my editor, Trisha Bora, who has been so patient.

I thank all the parents who believed in us to care for the development and growth of their children in one of our learning centres. It is not always easy to walk the less trodden path and to trust that it will lead to the correct destination.

I thank my colleagues who have stuck by me for years on this journey. It is said a dream can turn into dust or magic depending on the magic that rubs against it. I especially thank Divya Punjabi and Deepa Bushan for their inputs and Priya Gopal for all the research work for the book.

I thank my Mom, Zarna, and my Dad, Anil, for allowing me to live my blueprint.

I thank my brothers, Hiten and Kamal, for supporting and encouraging me every step of the way.

I thank my life partner, Kishore, who brings love, laughter, and learning into my life every day.

I thank my son, Drish, for being born to me.

A Note on the Author

Lina Ashar is the founder of Kangaroo Kids and Brainworks Pre-schools and Billabong High International Schools. She spent her primary school years in England and secondary school and college life in Australia.

She deeply believes that children should be taught not only to make a living but to make a life and, therefore, has evolved a system of education that uses the basis of neuroscience and energy science and develops the brain, heart, spirit, and soul of students. Her dream began in a tiny apartment in Bandra, Mumbai, with 13 students and has now grown to 170 schools, located in India, Dubai, and Maldives.

A Note on KKEL

Kangaroo Kids Education Ltd (KKEL) is a company that creates teaching and learning methodology delivery channels that teachers use in their classroom. These focus on creating high student engagement by ensuring all learning activities have purpose and meaning for the learner. KKEL believes that learning can only happen when there is willing attention and participation of the brain and this is what it constantly works on. KKEL knows that learning opportunities carefully crafted and presented in an integrated and high engagement manner can become an unending journey of discovery, knowledge creation, and growth.

KKEL believes the success of a school should not only be measured by test scores in exams but more on the success of students after they leave school. Exams are not the sole determinant of success. What then is the true role that education should play in a society? KKEL believes that education is not about burying children underneath volumes of incomprehensible formulae or facts. It is about creating enabling environments, ones that cater to all facets of development and creates students that are independent learners. It encourages questions, promotes curiosity, and makes a child a student for life.